vegetables

vegetables

MURDOCH BOOKS

Contents

Salads

Chicken and spring vegetable salad

600 g (1 lb 5 oz) boneless, skinless
  chicken breasts
½ lime, juiced
4 makrut (kaffir lime) leaves, shredded
½ onion, peeled
6 black peppercorns
175 g (6 oz/11 spears) asparagus
175 g (6 oz) broad (fava) beans,
  defrosted if frozen
225 g (8 oz) baby green beans

Lemon tarragon dressing
1 tablespoon olive oil
2 tablespoons lemon juice
2 tablespoons chopped tarragon
  leaves

Half-fill a large pot with water. Add the chicken, lime juice, makrut leaves, onion and peppercorns. Cover and bring to the boil, then reduce heat and simmer for 3 minutes. Turn off heat and leave chicken to cool in broth for at least 30 minutes — it will continue to cook.

Combine the dressing ingredients in a small bowl. Season lightly with salt and freshly ground black pepper, mix well and set aside. Snap woody ends off asparagus and discard. Bring another pot of water to the boil and add a pinch of salt. Add broad beans and cook for 1 minute, then add green beans and simmer for 1 minute. Now add the asparagus and cook for a further minute. Drain well and refresh under cold water. Drain well again.

Slice asparagus spears lengthways and place them in a serving dish with green beans. Remove skins from the broad beans and add them to serving dish. Remove cooled chicken from poaching liquid. Shred the breasts, then gently toss them through salad with the dressing. Serve at once.

Serves 4

Spinach and sweet potato salad with orange-sesame dressing

1 pitta bread
3 tablespoons olive oil
500 g (1 lb 2 oz) orange sweet potato
   unpeeled, cut into slices 1 cm
   (½ inch) thick
1 small orange
150 g (5 oz) baby spinach

Orange-sesame dressing
3 tablespoons olive oil
1 teaspoon sesame oil
2 tablespoons orange juice
1 teaspoon lemon juice
1 teaspoon orange zest, finely grated
1 garlic clove, crushed
2 teaspoons dijon mustard

Preheat a grill (broiler) to high. Cut off and discard the edge of the bread. Split the bread into 2 thin halves, and lightly brush all over with some of the oil. Toast under the grill until crisp and lightly browned. Reserve.

Toss sweet potato in the remaining oil and grill until soft and golden on both sides, 8–10 minutes. Transfer to a salad bowl.

Peel orange, removing all the pith. To fillet segments, hold orange over a bowl and use a knife to cut down either side of membranes. Put the segments in the bowl and add the spinach. Break up pitta crisps into small shards and put into the bowl. Toss lightly.

Put all the dressing ingredients in a small bowl and whisk to combine. Season with salt and freshly ground black pepper, to taste. Pour over the salad just before serving.

Serves 4

Warm vegetable and lentil salad

625 g (1 lb 6 oz) kipfler (fingerling)
  potatoes, scrubbed and halved
625 g (1 lb 6 oz) orange sweet
  potatoes, peeled and cut into 3 cm
  (1¼ inch) chunks
12 French shallots, peeled
350 g (12 oz/1 bunch) baby carrots,
  trimmed and scrubbed
1 large cauliflower, about 900 g (2 lb),
  cut into florets
80 ml (2½ fl oz/⅓ cup) olive oil
4 rindless bacon slices, about 160 g
  (5¾ oz) in total, chopped
400 g (14 oz) tinned lentils, rinsed and
  drained
100 g (3½ oz) baby English spinach
  leaves

Dressing
125 ml (4 fl oz/½ cup) chicken stock
125 ml (4 fl oz/½ cup) pouring
  (whipping) cream
1½ tablespoons white wine
25 g (1 oz) crumbled blue cheese
25 g (1 oz/¼ cup) grated parmesan
  cheese
125 g (4½ oz) chilled butter, chopped

Preheat the oven to 200°C (400°F/ Gas 6). Grease and line two baking trays with baking paper. Arrange the potato and sweet potato in a single layer on one of the trays, and spread the shallots, carrots and cauliflower on the other. Drizzle each with 1½ tablespoons of the oil and turn to coat. Season with salt and pepper and roast for 50–60 minutes, or until golden; remove the vegetables as they are cooked, as cooking times may vary. Set aside to cool for 10 minutes.

Meanwhile, heat the remaining oil in a non-stick frying pan over medium heat. Add the bacon and sauté for 6–7 minutes, or until golden. Drain the bacon on a paper towel, then transfer to a large bowl. Add the lentils, spinach and roasted vegetables and toss gently to combine. Keep warm.

To make the dressing, pour the stock, cream and wine into a pan and bring to the boil. Reduce heat to medium and simmer until reduced by half. Reduce heat to low, add the cheeses and stir to combine. Whisking constantly, add the butter a few pieces at a time, ensuring it has emulsified before adding more. Season to taste. Remove from the heat and cool to room temperature. Drizzle over the salad and gently toss to combine.

Serves 4-6

Mexicana salad

250 g (9 oz) black-eyed peas
250 g (9 oz/2½ cups) red kidney
  beans
500 g (1 lb 2 oz) orange sweet potato
1 large red onion, chopped
1 large green capsicum (pepper),
  chopped
3 ripe tomatoes, chopped
2 small handfuls chopped basil
3 flour tortillas
1 tablespoon oil
2 tablespoons grated parmesan
  cheese
60 g (2¼ oz/¼ cup) sour cream

Dressing
1 garlic clove, crushed
1 tablespoon lime juice
2 tablespoons olive oil

Guacamole
3 ripe avocados
2 tablespoons lemon juice
1 garlic clove, crushed
1 small red onion, chopped
1 small red chilli, chopped
60 g (2¼ oz/¼ cup) sour cream
2 tablespoons hot ready-made taco
  sauce

Soak the peas and beans in a bowl of cold water overnight. Drain and cook in a saucepan of rapidly boiling water for 30 minutes, or until just tender. Skim off any scum that appears on the surface during cooking. Do not overcook or they will become mushy. Drain and set aside to cool.

Chop the sweet potato into large pieces and cook in boiling water until tender. Drain and combine with the onion, capsicum, tomato, peas and beans. Stir in the basil.

To make the dressing, shake the ingredients in a screw-top jar until combined. Pour over the salad and toss to coat.

Preheat the oven to 180°C (350°F/ Gas 4). Using a small knife, cut large triangles out of the tortillas, brush each one lightly with the oil and sprinkle with parmesan. Bake for 5–10 minutes, or until they are crisp and golden.

To make the guacamole, mash the avocados with the lemon juice. Add the garlic, onion, chilli, sour cream and taco sauce and mix well. Pile the guacamole in the centre of the salad, top with the sour cream and arrange the triangle chips on top.

Serves 10-12

Roast mushroom and baby bean salad

600 g (1 lb 5 oz) field mushrooms,
  brushed clean
2 tablespoons olive oil
3 garlic cloves, crushed
2 tablespoons lemon juice
6 French shallots, root ends trimmed,
  skin left on
1½ tablespoons tarragon vinegar
2 teaspoons finely chopped tarragon
1 tablespoon finely chopped flat-leaf
  (Italian) parsley
200 g (7 oz) baby green beans,
  trimmed
2 handfuls rocket (arugula)

Preheat oven to 200°C (400°F/Gas 6). Place the mushrooms in a single layer in a large roasting tin. Add oil, garlic, lemon juice and shallots and toss until coated. Roast for around 30 minutes, occasionally spooning over the juices.

Remove from the oven and cool to room temperature. Slip shallots from their skins and discard skin. Pour the cooking juices into a large mixing bowl. Add tarragon vinegar, tarragon and parsley. Mix and season well.

Blanch beans in boiling salted water for 2 minutes, or until just tender. Drain well and, while still hot, add to the dressing. Allow to cool to room temperature.

Cut the mushrooms into quarters, or eighths if large, and add to the beans with the shallots and rocket. Gently toss together and serve.

Serves 4

Fresh beetroot and goat's cheese salad

1 kg (2 lb 4 oz) fresh beetroot (beets)
  (about 4 bulbs with leaves)
200 g (7 oz) green beans
100 g (4 oz) goat's cheese

Dressing
1 tablespoon red wine vinegar
2 tablespoons extra virgin olive oil
1 garlic clove, crushed
1 tablespoon drained capers, coarsely
  chopped

Trim leaves from the beetroot. Scrub the bulbs and wash the leaves well. Simmer bulbs in a large saucepan of boiling water, covered, for 30 minutes, or until tender when pierced with the point of a knife. (Cooking time may vary depending on size of the bulbs.)

Meanwhile, bring a saucepan of water to the boil, add the beans and cook for 3 minutes, or until tender. Remove with a slotted spoon and plunge into a bowl of cold water. Drain well. Add beetroot leaves to the same saucepan of boiling water and then cook for 3–5 minutes, or until the leaves and stems are tender. Drain, plunge into a bowl of water, then drain again well.

Cool the beetroot, then, wearing gloves, peel off the skins and cut the bulbs into thin wedges.

Divide the beans and beetroot (leaves and bulbs) among four serving plates. Crumble goat's cheese over the top.

Put all the dressing ingredients in a small bowl and whisk to combine. Season with salt and freshly ground black pepper, to taste. Pour over the salad just before serving.

Serves 4

Asparagus and mushroom salad

155 g (5½ oz/10 spears) asparagus
1 tablespoon wholegrain mustard
3 tablespoons orange juice
2 tablespoons lemon juice
1 tablespoon lime juice
1 tablespoon orange zest
2 teaspoons lemon zest
2 teaspoons lime zest
2 garlic cloves, crushed
90 g (3¼ oz/¼ cup) honey
400 g (14 oz) button mushrooms, halved
150 g (5½ oz) rocket (arugula) leaves
1 red capsicum (pepper), cut into strips

Snap the woody ends from the asparagus spears and cut in half on the diagonal. Cook in boiling water for 1 minute, or until just tender. Drain, plunge into cold water and set aside.

Place mustard, citrus juice and zest, garlic and honey in a large saucepan and season with freshly ground black pepper. Bring to the boil, then reduce the heat and add the mushrooms, tossing for 2 minutes. Cool.

Remove the mushrooms from the sauce with a slotted spoon. Return the sauce to the heat, bring to the boil, then reduce the heat and simmer for 3–5 minutes, or until reduced and syrupy. Cool slightly.

Toss the mushrooms, rocket leaves, capsicum and asparagus. Put on a plate and drizzle with the sauce.

Serves 4

Pumpkin, broccoli and chickpea salad with sweet yoghurt dressing

750 g (10 oz) jap or butternut pumpkin (squash), cut into large pieces
400 g (14 oz) tinned chickpeas, rinsed and drained
1 tablespoon soya bean oil
3 tablespoons sweet chilli sauce
300 g (11 oz) broccoli, cut into florets and steamed
50 g (2 oz) pepitas (pumpkin seeds), shelled
2 tablespoons chopped coriander (cilantro) leaves
2 tablespoons low-fat plain yoghurt

Preheat oven to 200°C (400°F/Gas 6). Put the pumpkin and chickpeas into a roasting tin, pour over the combined oil and 2 tablespoons of the sweet chilli sauce and toss to coat. Roast for 40 minutes or until the pumpkin is soft. Transfer to a salad bowl and fold through the cooked broccoli, pepitas and coriander.

Whisk together yoghurt and remaining sweet chilli sauce. Drizzle this mixture over salad and toss to combine.

Serves 4

Snap pea, carrot and cashew nut salad

175 g (6 oz) snap peas or snow peas
  (mangetout)
125 g (5 oz) carrots
150 g (5 oz) red cabbage
100 g (4 oz/²⁄₃ cups) cashews

Dressing
3 tablespoons sesame oil
2 tablespoons sunflower oil
2 tablespoons rice wine vinegar or
  white wine vinegar
1 teaspoon grated or finely chopped
  ginger
1 tablespoon tamari or light soy sauce

Slice the peas in half at an angle. Steam or microwave peas for 1 minute. Remove them and then leave to cool down. Next, peel the carrot into thin ribbons and finely shred red cabbage.

To make dressing, put the oil, vinegar, ginger and tamari or soy sauce into a salad bowl and whisk to combine.

Add vegetables and half the cashews to dressing and toss to coat. Scatter the remaining cashews on the salad.

Serves 4

Grilled vegetable salad

1 red onion
6 small eggplants (aubergines), about
    16 cm (6¼ inches) long
4 red capsicums (peppers)
4 orange capsicums (peppers)
1 tablespoon baby capers
80 ml (3 fl oz/⅓ cup) olive oil
1 tablespoon chopped flat-leaf (Italian)
    parsley
2 garlic cloves, finely chopped

Without slicing through the base, cut the onion from top to base into six sections, leaving it attached at base.

Put the onion on a barbecue (hotplate), or over an open-flamed grill (broiler) or gas stovetop, with eggplants and capsicums. Cook the vegetables over moderate heat for 10 minutes, turning occasionally, until the eggplants and the capsicum skins are blackened and blistered. Cool the capsicums in a plastic bag for about 10 minutes and set the onion and the eggplant aside. Dry-fry capers with a pinch of salt until crisp. Cut onion into its six sections and discard charred outer skins.

Peel skins off eggplants and remove the stalk. Cut from top to bottom into slices. Peel the capsicums, cut them in half and remove the seeds and membrane. Cut into wide slices.

Arrange all the vegetables on a large serving platter. Drizzle olive oil over them and season well. Scatter the parsley, garlic and capers over top. Serve cold.

Serves 4

Potato salad

600 g (1 lb 5 oz) potatoes, unpeeled,
  cut into bite-sized pieces
1 small onion, finely chopped
1 small green capsicum (pepper),
  chopped
2–3 celery stalks, finely chopped
1 large handful parsley, finely chopped

Dressing
185 g (6½ oz/¾ cup) mayonnaise
1–2 tablespoons vinegar or lemon
  juice
2 tablespoons sour cream

Cook the potato in a large saucepan of boiling water for 5 minutes, or until just tender (pierce with a sharp knife—if the potato yields easily it is ready). Drain and cool completely.

Combine the onion, capsicum, celery and parsley (reserving a little for garnishing) with the cooled potato in a large salad bowl.

To make the dressing, mix together the mayonnaise, vinegar and sour cream. Season with salt and freshly ground black pepper. Pour over the salad and toss gently to combine, without breaking the potato. Garnish with the remaining parsley.

Serves 4

Chickpea and roast vegetable salad

500 g (1 lb 2 oz) butternut pumpkin (squash), cubed
2 red capsicums (peppers), halved
4 slender eggplants (aubergine), cut in half lengthways
4 zucchini (courgettes), cut in half lengthways
4 onions, quartered
olive oil, for brushing
2 x 400 g (14 oz) tinned chickpeas, drained and rinsed
2 tablespoons chopped flat-leaf (Italian) parsley

Dressing
4 tablespoons olive oil
2 tablespoons lemon juice
1 garlic clove, crushed
1 tablespoon chopped thyme

Preheat the oven to 220°C (425°F/ Gas 7). Brush two baking trays with oil and lay out the vegetables in a single layer. Brush the vegetables lightly with oil.

Bake for 40 minutes, or until the vegetables are tender and begin to brown slightly on the edges. Cool. Remove the skins from the capsicum if you want. Chop the capsicum, eggplant and zucchini into pieces, then put the vegetables in a bowl with the chickpeas and half the parsley.

To make the dressing, whisk together all the dressing ingredients in a small bowl. Season, then toss with the vegetables. Leave for 30 minutes, then sprinkle with remaining parsley.

Serves 8

Brown rice, tuna and roasted vegetable salad

1 small red capsicum (pepper),
  roughly chopped
1 zucchini (courgette), thickly sliced
1 small onion, cut into wedges
2 tablespoons olive oil
140 g (5 oz/²/₃ cup) brown rice
  (see Note)
185 g (7 oz) tinned tuna chunks,
  drained

Orange and basil dressing
zest of 1 orange
2 tablespoons orange juice
2 tablespoons olive oil
3 tablespoons torn basil leaves

Preheat oven to 200°C (400°F/Gas 6).
Put the capsicum, zucchini and onion
in a baking dish. Pour the oil over the
top, season with salt and freshly
ground black pepper, then toss to
coat the vegetables with oil. Bake for
20 minutes or until lightly golden and
soft, stirring occasionally during cooking.

Meanwhile, cook the rice according to
the packet instructions. Drain well,
then rinse under cold water and drain
again. Leave to cool in a sieve over a
saucepan, fluffing up the grains with a
fork occasionally.

While the rice is cooling, put all the
orange and basil dressing ingredients
in a bowl and whisk well. Season with
salt and freshly ground black pepper.
Put the cooled rice in a bowl, then
stir in the tuna and all the roasted
vegetables. Pour over the dressing,
gently toss together, and divide salad
between two plates.

Serves 2

Note: You could also use leftover rice
for this recipe. You will need about
280 g (10 oz/1½ cups) of cold cooked
brown rice.

Spicy Indian lentil salad

210 g (7½ oz/1 cup) brown rice
185 g (6½ oz/1 cup) brown lentils
1 teaspoon turmeric
1 teaspoon ground cinnamon
6 cardamom pods
3 star anise
2 bay leaves
60 ml (2 fl oz/¼ cup) sunflower oil
1 tablespoon lemon juice
250 g (9 oz) broccoli florets
2 carrots, cut into matchsticks
1 onion, finely chopped
2 garlic cloves, crushed
1 red capsicum (pepper), finely
  chopped
1 teaspoon garam masala
1 teaspoon ground coriander
235 g (8½ oz/1⅔ cups) peas, frozen

Mint and yoghurt dressing
250 g (9 oz/1 cup) plain yoghurt
1 tablespoon lemon juice
1 tablespoon finely chopped mint
1 teaspoon cumin seeds

Put 750 ml (26 fl oz/3 cups) water with the rice, lentils, turmeric, cinnamon, cardamom, star anise and bay leaves in a saucepan. Stir to mix and bring to the boil. Reduce the heat, cover and simmer for 50–60 minutes. Remove the whole spices and discard. Transfer the mixture to a bowl. Whisk 2 tablespoons of the oil with the lemon juice and fork through the rice mixture.

Cook the broccoli and carrot until tender. Heat the remaining oil in a large saucepan and add the onion, garlic and capsicum. Stir-fry for 2–3 minutes, then add the garam masala and coriander. Cook 1–2 minutes. Meanwhile, cook the peas according to the packet instructions. Drain well.

Add vegetables and toss to coat. Add to the rice mixture and fork through to combine. Cover and refrigerate.

To make the dressing, mix all the ingredients, and season with salt and freshly ground black pepper. Serve the salad with the dressing.

Serves 6

Pumpkin with chilli and avocado

750 g (1 lb 10 oz) pumpkin (winter
squash)
1 large avocado

Dressing
1 small red onion
2 tablespoons olive oil
1 tablespoon chopped coriander
(cilantro) leaves
1 tablespoon chopped mint
2 teaspoons sweet chilli sauce
2 teaspoons balsamic vinegar
1 teaspoon soft brown sugar

Scrape the seeds from the inside of
the pumpkin. Cut the pumpkin into
slices and remove the skin. Cook in a
large saucepan of simmering water
until tender but still firm. Remove from
the heat and drain well.

To make the dressing, finely chop the
red onion. Combine the onion with the
remaining ingredients in a small bowl.

Cut avocado in half. Remove stone
using a sharp-bladed knife. Peel and
discard skin from the avocado, then
cut the flesh in thin slices.

Combine the warm pumpkin and
avocado in a serving bowl. Gently
toss the coriander dressing through.
Serve immediately.

Serves 6

Warm salad of Jerusalem artichoke, radicchio and pastrami

500 g (1 lb 2 oz) Jerusalem artichokes
juice of ½ lemon
pinch asafoetida
1 treviso radicchio
40 g (1½ oz/⅓ cup) golden walnut
   pieces
3 tablespoons walnut oil
1 small orange, zested and juiced
1 tablespoon shredded parsley
100 g (4 oz) pastrami slices, halved

Peel the artichokes. Cut any large ones to give pieces of roughly the same size. Put the artichokes in a non-reactive saucepan of boiling salted water with lemon juice and asafoetida. Simmer for 12 minutes, or until tender, then drain. When cool, slice the artichokes on the diagonal.

Preheat the grill (broiler) to hot. Trim off any coarse outer leaves from the radicchio and quarter it lengthways. Put the radicchio, cut side up, in a medium shallow heatproof dish, scatter the walnuts on top and then drizzle with half the oil. Grill (broil) for 1–2 minutes, or until leaves start to pucker and edges brown. Remove from the heat and set aside to cool for 2–3 minutes.

Cut off radicchio stems and return leaves to the dish. Add artichokes, orange juice and parsley and season with salt and freshly ground black pepper, to taste. Toss lightly. Scrunch the pastrami pieces into loose balls and arrange them among artichokes. Drizzle with remaining walnut oil and return to grill. Grill for 1–2 minutes, or until just beginning to brown. Top with orange zest and serve immediately.

Serves 4

Chargrilled vegetable salad with balsamic dressing

2 baby eggplants (aubergines)
2 large roma (plum) tomatoes
1 red capsicum (pepper)
$1/2$ green capsicum (pepper)
1 zucchini (courgette)
$2^1/2$ tablespoons olive oil
6 bocconcini or 12 small, fresh
  mozzarella cheeses
12 Ligurian olives
1 garlic clove, finely chopped
1 heaped teaspoon baby capers,
  rinsed and drained
$1/4$ teaspoon sugar
1 tablespoon balsamic vinegar

Cut the eggplants and tomatoes into quarters. Cut the capsicums in half lengthways, remove the seeds and membrane, then cut each half into thick strips. Thinly slice the zucchini on the diagonal.

Preheat a chargrill pan (griddle) or barbecue hotplate to high. Brush with $1/2$ tablespoon of the oil and cook the vegetables in batches for 2 minutes, or until slightly charred and golden, adding a little more oil as required. (The tomatoes are best cooked cut side down first.)

Put vegetables and cheese in a large bowl. Mix together the olives, garlic, capers, sugar and vinegar with the remaining oil, then pour over the salad and toss. Divide between two plates and serve.

Serves 2

Warm pea, broad bean and potato salad

500 g (1 lb 2 oz) new or small waxy
 potatoes
2 tablespoons olive oil
1 onion, finely chopped
75 g (3 oz) smoked pancetta or bacon
2 garlic cloves, chopped
250 g (9 oz) podded, tender peas
200 g (7 oz) podded, tender broad
 (fava) beans
2 sprigs basil, torn
1 tablespoon red wine
1 tablespoon low-fat yoghurt, optional

Boil potatos until soft, drain and set aside. Heat oil in a large saucepan and add onion and pancetta. Cook over a medium heat for 5 minutes until onions are soft and the pancetta slightly caramelised. Add the garlic, reduce the heat and cook for a further minute.

Cut potatos in half lengthways or in large slices if they are big. Add the potatoes to the onions and then gently cook, stirring periodically for around 5 minutes more.

Blanch the peas for a few minutes in boiling water until cooked, then remove with a slotted spoon and blanch the broad beans for a few minutes until soft. Drain and refresh broad beans in cold water. Remove the pale skin from any large broad beans and mix with peas. Add to the onions and stir briefly. Add basil and wine and cook for a further minute. Finally add the low-fat yoghurt if you are choosing to do so and remove from the heat. Serve on its own as a light meal or to accompany grilled chicken breast or lamb chops.

Serves 4

Cooked vegetable salad

1 small turnip
1 large onion
2 celery stalks
200 g (7 oz) button mushrooms
1 large carrot
1/2 red capsicum (pepper)
4 spring onions (scallions)
2 tablespoons sesame oil
1 tablespoon vegetable oil
2 garlic cloves, finely chopped
80 g (3 oz/1/2 cup) pine nuts, toasted
   (see Note)

Dressing
3 tablespoons soy sauce
1 tablespoon white vinegar
3 cm (1 1/4 inch) piece ginger, very
   finely sliced and cut into fine strips
1–2 teaspoons soft brown sugar

Cut turnip into thin strips. Slice the onion, celery stalks and the button mushrooms. Cut the carrot into fine strips. Cut the red capsicum in half, remove seeds and membrane and cut into fine strips. Chop spring onions.

Put turnip on a plate lined with paper towel. Sprinkle with 2 teaspoons of salt and then set aside for at least 20 minutes. Rinse turnip under cold water and pat dry with paper towel.

Heat combined oils in a large frying pan or wok and swirl to coat the base and side. Stir-fry the turnip, garlic and the onion for 3 minutes over medium heat, or until lightly golden. Add red capsicum, celery, mushrooms, carrot and spring onion and toss well. Cover and steam for 1 minute. Remove the the vegetables from the wok and set aside to cool.

To make dressing, combine all the ingredients in a bowl. Pour dressing over the cooled vegetables and toss. Arrange them on a serving plate and sprinkle with the pine nuts.

Serves 4

Note: Toast the pine nuts in a dry frying pan over medium heat, stirring constantly, until they are golden brown and fragrant.

Grilled vegetables with garlic mayonnaise

2 eggplants (aubergines), cut into thin
   slices
4 small leeks, white part only
4 small zucchini (courgettes)
2 red capsicums (peppers)
8 large flat mushrooms

Dressing
1 tablespoon balsamic vinegar
2 tablespoons dijon mustard
2 teaspoons dried oregano
250 ml (9 fl oz/1 cup) olive oil

Garlic mayonnaise
2 egg yolks
1 tablespoon lemon juice
2 garlic cloves, crushed
250 ml (9 fl oz/1 cup) olive oil
1 tablespoon snipped chives
1 tablespoon chopped flat-leaf (Italian)
   parsley

Sprinkle eggplant with salt and leave to stand for 30 minutes. Rinse under cold water, then pat dry with paper towel. Halve the leeks and zucchini lengthways. Cut the capsicum in half, remove the seeds and membrane and cut each half into four pieces.

To make dressing, combine vinegar, mustard and oregano in a bowl, then gradually whisk in the oil. Preheat the grill (broiler) to high. Place eggplant, leek, zucchini and capsicum in a single layer on a flat grill tray, then brush with some dressing. Cook under the grill on high for 5 minutes. Turn the vegetables once, brushing occasionally with dressing. Add the mushrooms to the grill tray and brush them with dressing. Continue cooking the vegetables for 10 minutes, or until tender, turning the mushrooms once.

To make the mayonnaise, put the egg yolks, lemon juice and garlic in a food processor or blender and blend for 5 seconds until combined. With the motor running, add oil slowly in a thin, steady stream until it is all added and mayonnaise is thick and creamy. Add the chives, parsley and 1 tablespoon water and blend until well combined. Serve with grilled vegetables.

Serves 8

Tunisian eggplant salad with preserved lemon

2 large eggplants (aubergines)
125 ml (4 fl oz/½ cup) olive oil
1 teaspoon cumin seeds
2 garlic cloves, very thinly sliced
1 tablespoon currants
1 tablespoon slivered almonds
6 small roma (plum) tomatoes,
    quartered lengthways
1 teaspoon dried oregano
½ preserved or salted lemon
4 red bird's eye chillies, halved
    lengthways and seeded
2 tablespoons lemon juice
1 large handful flat-leaf (Italian) parsley,
    chopped
extra virgin olive oil, to serve

Cut the eggplants into 2 cm (¾ inch) cubes, put in a large colander and sprinkle with 1–2 teaspoons salt. Set aside to drain in the sink for about 2–3 hours. Dry with paper towels.

Heat half of the olive oil in a large flameproof casserole dish over medium heat. Fry the eggplant in batches for 5–6 minutes, or until golden, adding more oil as needed.

Drain on crumpled paper towels.

Reduce heat and add any remaining oil to casserole dish, along with the cumin, garlic, currants and almonds. Fry for 20–30 seconds, or until garlic starts to colour. Add the tomato and oregano and then cook for 1 minute.

Remove from heat. Trim rind from the piece of preserved lemon and cut the rind into thin strips. Discard the flesh.

Return eggplant to casserole and add the chilli, the lemon juice, parsley and preserved lemon rind. Toss gently and season with freshly ground black pepper. Set aside at room temperature for 1 hour before serving. Check the seasoning, then drizzle with extra oil.

Serves 4

Warm radicchio salad with crushed tomato vinaigrette

4–5 tablespoons olive oil
6 garlic cloves, thinly sliced
7 roma (plum) tomatoes, cored and
  halved
3 tablespoons extra virgin olive oil
2 tablespoons red wine vinegar
1 teaspoon honey
900 g (2 lb) witlof (chicory/Belgian
  endive)
1 onion, halved and sliced
1 radicchio lettuce

Heat half the olive oil in a small frying pan, add the garlic and fry over moderately high heat for a few minutes, or until lightly browned. Drain on paper towels.

Heat a little more olive oil in the frying pan and cook the tomatoes, cut side down, over moderate heat until browned and very soft. Turn to brown the other side. Transfer to a bowl to cool, then peel and discard the skins. Coarsely mash the flesh with a fork.

To make the vinaigrette, whisk together about half of the crushed tomatoes, the extra virgin olive oil, vinegar and honey. Season with salt and freshly ground black pepper.

Trim the coarse stems from the witlof, wash the leaves very well and drain. Cut into short lengths. Heat the rest of the olive oil in the frying pan, add the onion and cook until transparent. Add the witlof and stir until just wilted. Add the remaining tomatoes and stir until well combined. Season with salt and freshly ground black pepper.

Tear radicchio leaves into smaller pieces. Toss through the chicory mixture. Transfer to a serving bowl, drizzle with the vinaigrette and sprinkle with the garlic. Serve immediately.

Serves 4

Roasted vegetables with pan-fried garlic breadcrumbs

3 zucchini (courgettes), sliced
225 g (8 oz) button mushrooms, larger ones halved
1 red onion, cut into 8 wedges
1 red capsicum (pepper), diced
3 tablespoons olive oil
1 garlic clove, crushed
40 g (1½ oz/½ cup) breadcrumbs, made from day-old bread

Dressing
1 tablespoon olive oil
2 tablespoons ready-made pesto
1 tablespoon lemon juice

Preheat oven to 200°C (400°F/Gas 6). Put all vegetables in a large baking dish. Drizzle over 2 tablespoons of the oil, add salt and freshly ground black pepper and shake pan to coat all the vegetables in the oil. Roast for 30 minutes, or until all the vegetables are tender.

Combine the dressing ingredients in a large serving bowl. Add the roasted vegetables, toss gently and leave for 10 minutes for the flavours to absorb.

Heat the remaining oil in a frying pan and fry the garlic over medium heat for about 30 seconds. Increase the heat, add the breadcrumbs and fry for 2–3 minutes, or until golden, shaking the pan and stirring the crumbs. Toss the toasted breadcrumbs through the salad and serve.

Serves 4

Chargrilled cauliflower salad with sesame dressing

Sesame dressing
3 tablespoons tahini
1 garlic clove, crushed
60 ml (2 fl oz/¼ cup) seasoned rice
   wine vinegar
1 tablespoon vegetable oil
1 teaspoon lime juice
¼ teaspoon sesame oil

1 medium head cauliflower
12 garlic cloves, crushed
2 tablespoons vegetable oil
2 baby cos (romaine) lettuces, washed
   well and drained
50 g (1¾ oz) picked watercress
   leaves, washed well and drained
2 teaspoons sesame seeds, toasted
1 tablespoon finely chopped parsley

Preheat the chargrill pan (griddle) or barbecue hotplate to medium heat. In a medium non-metallic bowl, place the tahini, garlic, rice wine vinegar, vegetable oil, lime juice, sesame oil and 1 tablespoon water. Whisk together thoroughly until well combined, and season to taste.

Cut the cauliflower in half, and then into 1 cm (½ inch) wedges. Place on a tray and gently rub with the garlic and vegetable oil. Season well. Chargrill the cauliflower pieces until golden on both sides and cooked through. Remove from the chargrill pan.

Arrange the cos leaves and watercress on a serving platter and top with the chargrilled cauliflower slices. Drizzle the dressing over the top and garnish with the sesame seeds and parsley. Serve immediately.

Serves 4

Gado gado

6 new potatoes
2 carrots, cut into thick batons
250 g (9 oz) snake beans, cut into
   long lengths
2 tablespoons peanut oil
250 g (9 oz) firm tofu, cubed
2 Lebanese (short) cucumbers, cut
   into batons
1 large red capsicum (pepper), cut
   into batons
100 g (3½ oz) bean sprouts
5 hard-boiled eggs

Peanut sauce
1 tablespoon peanut oil
1 onion, finely chopped
150 g (5½ oz/⅔ cup) peanut butter
60 ml (2 fl oz/¼ cup) kecap manis
2 tablespoons ground coriander
2 teaspoons chilli sauce
185 ml (6 fl oz/¾ cup) coconut cream
1 teaspoon grated palm sugar
   (jaggery)
1 tablespoon lemon juice

Boil the potatoes until tender. Drain
and cool slightly. Cut into quarters.
Cook the carrot and beans separately
in boiling water until just tender.
Plunge into iced water, then drain.

Heat the oil in a non-stick frying pan
and cook the tofu in batches. Drain
on paper towels.

To make the peanut sauce, heat the
oil in a frying pan over low heat and
cook the onion for about 5 minutes.
Add the peanut butter, kecap manis,
coriander, chilli sauce and coconut
cream. Bring to the boil, reduce the
heat and simmer for 5 minutes. Stir
in the palm sugar and juice until the
sugar has dissolved. Arrange the
vegetables and tofu on a plate. Halve
the eggs and place in the centre.
Serve with the sauce.

Serves 4

Potato, spinach, white bean and avocado salad

6 desiree or other all-purpose
  potatoes, washed
2 red capsicums (peppers), halved
  and seeded
100 g (3½ oz) snow peas
  (mangetout), trimmed
3 tablespoons extra virgin olive oil
2 garlic cloves, finely chopped
1 teaspoon fish sauce
1 teaspoon grated palm sugar
  (jaggery) or soft brown sugar
125 ml (4 fl oz/½ cup) lime juice
400 g (14 oz) tinned cannellini beans,
  drained and rinsed
50 g (1¾ oz) baby English spinach
1 large handful coriander (cilantro)
  leaves
2 avocados, diced
1 French shallot, finely chopped
1 small red chilli, seeded and finely
  chopped

Line a double steamer with baking paper and punch with holes. Lay the potatoes in the bottom tray and the capsicum in the top. Cover with a lid. Sit the steamer over a saucepan or wok of boiling water and steam for 30 minutes, or until the potatoes are tender. Put the capsicum in a plastic bag to cool, then peel and slice into strips.

Lightly steam the snow peas for 1–2 minutes, then slice into strips.

Meanwhile, peel the potatoes while they are still hot and cut into 1 cm (½ inch) rounds. Combine the oil, garlic, fish sauce, sugar and 3 tablespoons of the lime juice in a cup. Put the potato rounds in a bowl and pour on half the dressing.

Put the capsicum, snow peas, cannellini beans, spinach and coriander in a large bowl. Pour on the remaining dressing and toss to combine. In a separate bowl combine the avocado, shallot, chilli and remaining lime juice.

To serve, divide the potato slices among serving plates. Pile the bean salad over the potatoes and top with a good dollop of the avocado mixture.

Serves 4–6

Bean and vegetable salad with chilli and black vinegar dressing

2 fennel bulbs, trimmed and sliced lengthways
125 g (4½ oz/⅔ cup) baby corn, halved on the diagonal
150 g (5½ oz) snow peas (mangetout), trimmed and halved on the diagonal
400 g (14 oz) tinned pinto or borlotti (cranberry) beans, drained and rinsed
100 g (3½ oz/1 small bunch) baby rocket (arugula)
40 g (1½ oz/1 heaped cup) snow pea (mangetout) sprouts

Black vinegar dressing
4 tablespoons olive oil
3 tablespoons black vinegar (see Tip)
1 tablespoon rice vinegar
2 tablespoons finely chopped coriander (cilantro) leaves
1 small red chilli, seeded and finely chopped

Line a steamer with baking paper and punch with holes. Put the fennel and baby corn in the steamer and cover with a lid. Sit the steamer over a saucepan or wok of boiling water and steam for 5 minutes. Add the snow peas and beans and steam for a further 5 minutes. Transfer to a bowl, making sure you leave any condensed steaming liquid on the baking paper.

Meanwhile, to make the dressing, whisk together the oil, black vinegar and rice vinegar until well combined. Season well. Stir in coriander and chilli.

Pour half the dressing over the vegetables, toss well, then leave for 5 minutes or to cool completely. Arrange the rocket leaves on a serving platter and drizzle with the remaining dressing. Spoon on the dressed vegetables and scatter the snow pea sprouts over the top.

Serves 4

Tip: Black vinegar is similar to balsamic, but has a slightly smoky flavour. Buy it from Asian food stores or in the Asian section of larger supermarkets.

Fresh tuna Niçoise

4 eggs
600 g (1 lb 5 oz) waxy potatoes, such
as kipfler or pink fir apple, peeled
200 g (7 oz) green beans
700 g (1 lb 9 oz) tuna steaks, cut to
2 cm (¾ inch) thick
90 ml (3 fl oz) olive oil
2 tablespoons red wine vinegar
2 tablespoons chopped flat-leaf
(Italian) parsley
20 cherry tomatoes, halved
1 small red onion, thinly sliced
100 g (3½ oz/¾ cup) pitted black
olives

Place the eggs in a saucepan of cold water, bring to the boil, then reduce the heat and simmer for 4 minutes. Cool the eggs under cold running water, then shell and quarter.

Return the water to the boil, add the potatoes, then reduce the heat and simmer for 12 minutes, or until tender. Remove. Add the beans to the pan and cook for 3–4 minutes, or until tender but still bright green. Drain, refresh under cold water and cut in half. Slice the potatoes thickly.

Rub pepper on both sides of the tuna. Sear on a chargrill pan, barbecue hotplate, or in a frying pan, for 2 minutes on each side for rare, or until still pink in the middle. Cool slightly, then slice.

Combine the oil, vinegar and parsley in a cup. Gently toss the potato, beans, tomatoes, onion and olives in a bowl, and season. Add three-quarters of the dressing and toss well. Divide among four bowls, top with the tuna and egg, and drizzle with the remaining dressing.

Serves 4

Vietnamese chicken salad

400 g (14 oz) boneless, skinless
  chicken breasts
1 lemongrass stem, white part only,
  finely chopped
1 tablespoon fish sauce
2 teaspoons sugar
2 tablespoons lime juice
1½ tablespoons sweet chilli sauce
200 g (7 oz) Chinese cabbage, thinly
  sliced
1 carrot, cut into ribbons with a
  vegetable peeler
½ small red onion, sliced
1 large handful coriander (cilantro)
  leaves
1 large handful roughly chopped mint
2 tablespoons coriander (cilantro)
  leaves, extra
2 tablespoons chopped peanuts
1 tablespoon crisp fried shallots

Place the chicken and lemongrass in a deep frying pan of lightly salted water. Bring to the boil, then reduce the heat and simmer gently for 8–10 minutes, or until the chicken is just cooked through. Drain and keep warm.

Place the fish sauce, sugar, lime juice and sweet chilli sauce in a small saucepan and stir over medium heat for 1 minute, or until the sugar has dissolved. Remove from the heat.

Place the cabbage, carrot, onion, coriander and mint in a large bowl, and toss together well. Drizzle over three-quarters of the warmed dressing, toss to combine and transfer to a serving platter.

Slice the chicken thinly on the diagonal, arrange over the top of the salad and drizzle with the remaining dressing. Garnish with the extra coriander leaves, chopped peanuts and crisp fried shallots. Serve immediately.

Serves 4

Variation: Instead of Chinese cabbage, a large green papaya may be used. Remove skin and finely shred the fruit.

Beef, parsnip, prune and prosciutto salad

Dressing
1½ tablespoons dijon mustard
1 egg yolk
3 tablespoons red wine vinegar
250 ml (9 fl oz/1 cup) extra virgin
    olive oil
4 tablespoons torn basil leaves

125 ml (4 fl oz/½ cup) dry Marsala
24 pitted prunes
1 kg (2 lb 4 oz) piece of beef fillet,
    trimmed
90 ml (3 fl oz) olive oil
600 g (1 lb 5 oz) parsnips, peeled and
    cut into rounds 5 mm (¼ inch) thick
2 red onions, peeled and cut into
    wedges
100 g (3½ oz) thinly sliced prosciutto
1 radicchio, outer leaves discarded,
    leaves washed, dried and torn into
    pieces
150 g (5½ oz/1 medium bunch) rocket
    (arugula), trimmed, washed and
    dried

To make the dressing, put the mustard, yolk and vinegar in a bowl and whisk well. Whisking constantly, add the olive oil in a very slow, steady stream. Season to taste with sea salt and freshly ground black pepper, then add the basil and stir to combine.

Bring the Marsala to the boil in a small saucepan. Add the prunes, remove from heat and stir. Cover and set aside.

Preheat the oven to 220°C (425°F/ Gas 7). Using kitchen string, tie the beef at 5 cm (2 inch) intervals. Heat 2 tablespoons of the oil in a pan, add the beef and cook over high heat, turning often, until browned all over. Season with salt and pepper, then transfer the pan to the oven and roast the beef for 17–20 minutes. Remove from oven and set aside.

Reduce the oven to 200°C (400°F/ Gas 6). Put the parsnip and onion in a roasting tin, add the remaining olive oil and toss to coat. Roast until tender, turning once. Drain on paper towels, then let cool to room temperature.

Remove the string from the beef. Thinly slice and place in a large bowl with the prunes, roasted vegetables, prosciutto, radicchio and rocket and toss well. Serve immediately.

Serves 6

Lamb with roasted tomatoes

1 tablespoon red wine vinegar
½ Lebanese (short) cucumber, finely
  diced
100 g (3 ¾ oz) Greek-style yoghurt
2 teaspoons chopped mint
½ teaspoon ground cumin
80 ml (2½ fl oz/⅓ cup) olive oil
6 vine-ripened tomatoes
4 garlic cloves, finely chopped
1 tablespoon chopped oregano
1 tablespoon chopped parsley
600 g (1 lb 5 oz/38 spears) asparagus,
  trimmed
2 lamb backstraps or loin fillets
  (500 g/1 lb 2 oz)

Combine the vinegar, cucumber, yoghurt, chopped mint, cumin and 1 tablespoon of olive oil in a small cup.

Preheat the oven to 180°C (350°F/ Gas 4). Cut the tomatoes in half and scoop out the seeds. Combine the garlic, oregano and parsley, and sprinkle into the tomato shells.

Place the tomatoes on a rack in a baking tin. Drizzle them with 1 tablespoon of the olive oil and roast for 1 hour. Remove from the oven, cut each piece in half again and keep warm. Place the asparagus in the roasting tin, drizzle with another tablespoon of olive oil, season and roast for 10 minutes.

Meanwhile, heat the remaining oil in a frying pan. Season the lamb well and cook over medium–high heat for 5 minutes on each side, then set aside to rest.

Remove the asparagus from the oven and arrange on a serving plate. Top with the tomato. Slice the lamb on the diagonal and arrange on top of the tomato. Drizzle with the dressing and serve immediately.

Serves 4

Salami pasta salad

1 red capsicum (pepper)
1 green capsicum (pepper)
4 celery stalks
1 fennel bulb, trimmed
1 red onion
200 g (7 oz) thickly sliced pepper-
    coated salami
1 large handful chopped flat-leaf
    (Italian) parsley
300 g (10½ oz) mixed coloured
    fettucine, broken into short pieces

Dressing
125 ml (4 fl oz/½ cup) olive oil
3 tablespoons lemon juice
2½ tablespoons dijon mustard
1 teaspoon sugar
1 garlic clove, crushed

Slice the red and green capsicums into strips and place them in a large bowl. Slice the celery and add to the bowl. Cut the fennel and onion in half, then slice and add to the bowl. Cut the salami into strips and add to the bowl along with the parsley.

Cook the fettucine in a large saucepan of rapidly boiling salted water until just tender. Drain and rinse in cold water. Transfer the cooked pasta to the bowl and mix thoroughly with the capsicum, celery, fennel, onion, parsley and salami.

To make the dressing, combine the olive oil, lemon juice, mustard, sugar and crushed garlic, and season to taste with salt and plenty of cracked pepper. Pour over the salad and toss well to coat.

Serves 8

Risoni and broccoli salad with fresh herb dressing

8 garlic cloves, unpeeled
2 tablespoons extra virgin olive oil
125 g (4½ oz) whole egg mayonnaise
100 g (3½ oz) crème fraîche
80 g (2¾ oz) pesto
2 tablespoons lemon juice
250 g (9 oz) broccoli florets
400 g (14 oz) risoni (rice-shaped pasta)
100 g (3½ oz) toasted slivered almonds
1 tablespoon finely chopped parsley
1 tablespoon finely snipped chives

shaved parmesan cheese

Preheat the oven to 180°C (350°F/ Gas 4). Toss the garlic cloves in the olive oil and bake for 45 minutes, or until they are soft and golden.

Squeeze two of the garlic cloves from their skins and place in a food processor. Add the mayonnaise, crème fraîche, pesto and lemon juice, and process until just combined, then set aside until required.

Meanwhile, steam the broccoli florets for a few minutes, then refresh under cold water and drain well. Bring a large saucepan of water to the boil, then add 1 teaspoon of salt and the risoni, and cook for 8–10 minutes, or until *al dente*. Drain.

Add the almonds, dressing, parsley and chives to the risoni while still warm, and toss with the broccoli in a large bowl. Serve in deep salad bowls garnished with shaved parmesan and a roasted garlic clove on each portion.

Serves 6

Variation: Adding some cooked, peeled king prawns will make this salad extra special.

Cucumber and olive salad

4 Lebanese (short) cucumbers
1 red onion
3 teaspoons caster (superfine) sugar
1 tablespoon red wine vinegar
3 tablespoons olive oil
1/2 teaspoon finely crumbled dried
   za'atar, or 1 teaspoon finely
   chopped lemon thyme
90 g (3 1/4 oz/1/2 cup) black olives
flat bread, to serve

Wash the cucumbers and dry with paper towel. Do not peel the cucumbers if the skins are tender. Coarsely grate the cucumbers, mix the grated flesh with 1/2 teaspoon salt and leave to drain well.

Halve the onion and chop it finely. Add to the cucumber, along with the sugar and toss together.

In a small bowl, beat the red wine vinegar with the olive oil, then add the za'atar, and freshly ground black pepper, to taste. Whisk the ingredients together and pour over the cucumber. Cover and chill for 15 minutes. Scatter with olives and serve with flat bread.

Serves 4

Multicoloured salad

6 baby beetroot (beets)
200 g (7 oz/1 bunch) broccolini, cut
  into 4 cm (1½ inch) lengths
6 new potatoes
6 red coral lettuce leaves, torn
1 roasted red capsicum (pepper), cut
  into 1 cm (½ inch) strips (see Tip)
1 roasted yellow capsicum (pepper),
  cut into 1 cm (½ inch) strips
  (see Tip)
125 g (4½ oz) yellow teardrop
  tomatoes, halved
125 g (4½ oz) cherry tomatoes,
  halved
½ red onion, finely sliced
1 tablespoon chopped tarragon
3 tablespoons extra virgin olive oil
2 tablespoons balsamic vinegar
½ teaspoon wholegrain mustard

Wrap each beetroot in foil and place in a steamer with the broccolini and potatoes. Cover and sit the steamer over a saucepan or wok of boiling water. Remove the broccolini after 2–3 minutes, or when just cooked, the potatoes after about 20 minutes, or when easily pierced with a skewer, and the beetroot after 40 minutes, or when easily pierced (replenish the water if necessary). Allow the vegetables to cool then remove the skin from the beetroot and potatoes and cut into quarters.

Arrange the lettuce on a platter and top with the beetroot, broccolini, potato, red and yellow capsicum, tomatoes, onion and tarragon.

Combine the oil, vinegar and mustard in a screw-top jar and season with salt and freshly ground black pepper. Shake well, then pour the dressing over the salad.

Serves 6

Tip: To roast capsicums, cut them into large flattish pieces and remove the membrane and seeds. Cook, skin side up, under a hot grill (broiler) until the skin blackens and blisters. Cool in a plastic bag, then peel and slice.

Sweet potato, squash and spinach salad

800 g (1 lb 12 oz) orange sweet
potato, cut into 1 cm (1/2 inch) thick
rounds, then halved or quartered
350 g (12 oz) baby (pattypan) squash,
sliced lengthways into 4 pieces
150 g (5 1/2 oz) baby English spinach
60 g (2 1/4 oz/1/2 cup) slivered almonds,
toasted
6 bulb spring onions (scallions), finely
sliced (including some of the green
part)
1 large handful coriander (cilantro)
leaves

Dressing
1/4 preserved lemon, flesh and pith
removed, zest finely chopped
2 teaspoons honey
1 garlic clove, finely chopped
1/2 teaspoon ground cumin
1/2 teaspoon ground coriander
2 tablespoons apple cider vinegar
3 tablespoons olive oil

Line a large steamer with baking
paper and punch with holes. Put the
sweet potato on top and cover with a
lid. Sit the steamer over a saucepan or
wok of boiling water and steam for
12 minutes, or until tender. Carefully
remove the potato and set aside to
cool a little. Steam the squash for
about 3 minutes, or until almost
tender. Remove and set aside to
cool a little.

Meanwhile, to make the dressing, mix
together the preserved lemon, honey,
garlic, cumin, coriander and vinegar
in a bowl and season with salt and
freshly ground black pepper. Pour the
oil into the bowl in a steady stream
and stir well to combine.

Gently combine the sweet potato,
squash, spinach, almonds, spring
onion and coriander in a bowl. Pour
on the dressing and gently toss.
Transfer to a serving platter and serve.

Serves 4

Caponata

1 kg (2 lb 4 oz) eggplant (aubergine),
  cubed
185 ml (6 fl oz/$^3/_4$ cup) olive oil
200 g (7 oz) zucchini (courgettes),
  cubed
1 red capsicum (pepper), thinly sliced
2 onions, finely sliced
4 celery stalks, sliced
400 g (13 oz) tinned chopped
  tomatoes
3 tablespoons red wine vinegar
2 tablespoons sugar
2 tablespoons drained and rinsed
  capers
24 green olives, pitted (see Note)
2 tablespoons pine nuts, toasted

Put the eggplant in a colander,
sprinkle with salt and leave to drain.

Heat 3 tablespoons of the oil in a large
frying pan and fry the zucchini and
capsicum for 5–6 minutes, or until the
zucchini is lightly browned. Transfer to
a bowl. Add a little more oil to the pan
and gently fry the onion and celery for
6–8 minutes, or until softened but not
brown. Transfer to the bowl.

Rinse the eggplant and pat dry. Add
3 tablespoons of the oil to the pan,
increase the heat and brown the
eggplant in batches. Keep adding
more oil to each batch. Drain on paper
towels and set aside.

Remove any excess oil from the frying
pan and return the vegetables to the
pan, except the eggplant.

Add 3 tablespoons water and the
tomatoes. Reduce the heat, simmer
for 10 minutes. Add the remaining
ingredients and eggplant and mix well.
Remove from the heat and cool.
Cover and leave for 24 hours in the
refrigerator. Add some pepper, and
more vinegar if needed.

Serves 8

Note: Green olives stuffed with red
pimentos can be used instead of
pitted green olives.

Smoked trout, fennel and potato salad

750 g (1 lb 10 oz) new potatoes
125 g (4½ oz/½ cup) mayonnaise
1½ tablespoons lime juice
1 teaspoon finely grated lime zest
3 tablespoons chopped flat-leaf
    (Italian) parsley
sea salt, to taste
1 tablespoon red wine vinegar
2 teaspoons caster (superfine) sugar
4 tablespoons olive oil
1 large fennel bulb, trimmed and outer
    skin removed
1 red onion, finely sliced
100 g (3½ oz/1 small bunch) baby
    rocket (arugula)
1 tablespoon capers, rinsed and
    squeezed dry
350 g (12 oz) whole smoked trout,
    skin and bones removed, flesh
    shredded into bite-sized pieces

Put the potatoes in a steamer and cover with a lid. Sit the steamer over a saucepan or wok of boiling water and steam for 20–25 minutes, or until just tender (take care not to overcook them or they will fall apart when sliced). Drain and allow to cool for 5 minutes, then cut the potatoes into 1–2 cm (½–¾ inch) thick slices.

Meanwhile, combine the mayonnaise, lime juice, lime zest and parsley and season with sea salt and freshly ground black pepper.

Combine the vinegar, sugar, some sea salt and freshly ground black pepper in a large bowl and whisk until the sugar has dissolved. Slowly add the oil and continue to whisk until all the ingredients are combined. If the mixture is too thick, thin it down with 1–2 tablespoons of warm water, or until it reaches a drizzling consistency.

Add the fennel, onion, rocket and capers to the vinaigrette. Add the potatoes and half the smoked trout and toss gently to combine.

Divide the salad among serving plates and top with the remaining smoked trout. Drizzle the lime mayonnaise over each portion and serve with crusty bread.

Serves 4–6

Fiery barbecue lamb salad

600 g (1 lb 5 oz) butternut pumpkin
(squash), peeled and cut into 3 cm
(1¼ inch) wedges
1 garlic bulb
3 tablespoons olive oil
2 x 200 g (7 oz) lamb backstraps or
loin fillets
100 g (3½ oz) baby English spinach
leaves
95 g (3¼ oz) pitted green olives
80 g (2¾ oz/⅔ cup) goat's cheese,
crumbled
3 tablespoons olive oil
1 tablespoon lemon juice

Spice mix
2 teaspoons cayenne pepper
2 teaspoons mild paprika
1 teaspoon mustard powder
1 teaspoon ground coriander
1 teaspoon salt
¼ teaspoon freshly cracked black
pepper
½ teaspoon ground cumin
1 teaspoon dried thyme
1 teaspoon soft brown sugar

Preheat the oven to 190°C (375°F/
Gas 5). Put the pumpkin and
garlic bulb onto a roasting pan
lined with baking paper, drizzle with
1 tablespoon of the olive oil and
season with salt and pepper. Bake for
45–50 minutes, or until the garlic is
soft and the pumpkin is golden.

In a small bowl, combine the
ingredients for the spice mix. Lightly
coat the lamb with 1 tablespoon of the
mix, reserving the remainder in an
airtight container for future use.

Heat a barbecue grill plate or chargrill
pan over medium–high heat. Drizzle
the lamb with 1 tablespoon of oil and
cook for 2–3 minutes on each side for
medium–rare, or until cooked to your
liking. Cover with foil and set aside to
rest for 5 minutes before slicing.

Slice the end off the garlic bulb and
squeeze the garlic flesh into a food
processor. Purée with half the oil until
smooth. Add the remaining oil and
purée again until combined. Stir in the
lemon juice and 1 tablespoon of hot
water and season to taste.

In a large bowl, toss the spinach,
pumpkin, lamb, olives, goat's cheese
and dressing together. Divide among
four plates and serve immediately.

Serves 4

Tomato, onion and capsicum salad

2 green capsicums (peppers)
4 tomatoes
1 red onion
1 garlic clove, finely chopped
1 tablespoon finely chopped flat-leaf
  (Italian) parsley
80 ml (2½ fl oz/⅓ cup) olive oil
1 tablespoon red wine vinegar

Cut the capsicums into large flattish pieces and remove the seeds and white membranes. Place the pieces, skin side up, under a grill (broiler) and grill (broil) until the skin blackens. Turn them over and cook for 2–3 minutes on the fleshy side. Remove the cooked capsicum and place in a plastic bag, tuck the end of the bag underneath and leave to steam in the bag until cool enough to handle. Remove the blackened skin and cut the flesh into short strips. Place in a bowl.

Peel the tomatoes. To do this, score a cross on the base of each one using a knife. Put the tomatoes in a bowl of boiling water for 20 seconds, then plunge into a bowl of cold water to cool. Remove from the water and peel the skin away from the cross – it should slip off easily. Cut the tomatoes in half crossways and squeeze out the seeds. Dice the tomatoes and add to the capsicum. Halve the onion lengthways and remove the root. Cut into slender wedges. Add to the bowl, along with the garlic and parsley.

Beat the olive oil with the red wine vinegar and add ½ teaspoon salt and a good grinding of black pepper. Pour the dressing over the salad ingredients and toss well.

Serves 4

Carrot and orange salad

3 sweet oranges
500 g (1 lb 2 oz) carrots
2 tablespoons lemon juice
1 teaspoon ground cinnamon, plus
   extra, to serve
1 tablespoon caster (superfine) sugar
1 tablespoon orange flower water
small mint leaves, to serve

Cut off the tops and bases of the oranges. Cut the peel off using a sharp knife, removing all traces of pith and cutting through the outer membranes to expose the flesh. Holding the orange over a bowl to catch the juice, segment the oranges by cutting between the membranes. Remove the seeds and place the segments in the bowl. Squeeze the remains of the orange to extract all the juice. Pour the juice into another bowl.

Peel the carrots and cut into thin batons using a sharp knife. Put the carrots in the bowl with the orange juice. Add the lemon juice, cinnamon, sugar, orange flower water and a small pinch of salt. Stir well to combine. Cover the carrot mixture and oranges and refrigerate until required.

Just before serving, drain off the accumulated juice from the oranges and arrange the segments around the edge of a serving dish. Pile the carrot batons in the centre and top with the mint leaves. Dust the oranges lightly with a little of the extra cinnamon.

Serves 6

Russian salad

Mayonnaise
2 egg yolks
1 teaspoon dijon mustard
125 ml (4 fl oz/½ cup) extra virgin
olive oil
2 tablespoons lemon juice
2 small garlic cloves, crushed

3 bottled artichoke hearts
3 all-purpose potatoes, such as
desiree, unpeeled
100 g (3½ oz) baby green beans,
trimmed and cut into 1 cm (½ inch)
lengths
1 large carrot, cut into 1 cm (½ inch)
dice
125 g (4½ oz) fresh peas
30 g (1 oz) cornichons, chopped
2 tablespoons baby capers, rinsed
and drained
4 anchovy fillets, finely chopped
10 black olives, each cut into 3 slices
whole black olives, extra, to garnish

To make the mayonnaise, use electric beaters to beat the egg yolks with the mustard and ¼ teaspoon salt until creamy. Gradually add the oil in a fine stream, beating constantly until all the oil has been added. Add the lemon juice, garlic and 1 teaspoon boiling water and beat for 1 minute, or until well combined. Season to taste.

Cut each artichoke into quarters. Rinse the potatoes, cover with salted cold water and bring to a gentle simmer. Cook for 15–20 minutes, or until tender when pierced with a knife. Drain and allow to cool slightly. Peel and set aside. When the potatoes are completely cool, cut into 1 cm (½ inch) dice.

Blanch the beans in salted boiling water until tender but still firm to the bite. Refresh in cold water, then drain thoroughly. Repeat with the carrot and peas.

Set aside a small quantity of each vegetable, including the cornichons, for the garnish and season to taste. Put the remainder in a bowl with the capers, anchovies and sliced olives. Add mayonnaise, toss to combine and season. Arrange on a serving dish and garnish with the reserved vegetables and the whole olives.

Serves 4–6

Soups

Jerusalem artichoke and roast garlic soup

1 garlic bulb
2 tablespoons butter
1 tablespoon olive oil
1 onion, chopped
1 leek, white part only, washed and
   chopped
1 celery stalk, chopped
700 g (1 lb 9 oz) Jerusalem
   artichokes, peeled and chopped
1 small potato, chopped
1.5 litres (6 cups) vegetable or chicken
   stock
olive oil, to serve
finely snipped chives, to serve

Preheat the oven to 200°C (400°F/ Gas 6). Slice the base from the bulb of garlic, wrap it in foil and roast for 30 minutes, or until soft. When cool enough to handle, remove from the foil and slip the cloves from the skin. Set aside.

In a large heavy-based saucepan, heat the butter and oil. Add the onion, leek and celery and a large pinch of salt, and cook for 10 minutes, or until soft. Add the Jerusalem artichokes, potato and garlic and cook for a further 10 minutes. Pour in the stock, bring the mixture to the boil, then reduce the heat and simmer for 30 minutes, or until the vegetables are soft.

Allow the liquid to cool slightly, then purée in a blender until smooth, and season well. Serve with a drizzle of olive oil and some chives. Delicious with warm crusty bread.

Serves 4

Green soup with pistou

60 ml (2 fl oz/¼ cup) olive oil
1 onion, finely chopped
2 garlic cloves, crushed
1 celery stalk, chopped
1 zucchini (courgette), cut into
   1 cm (½ inch) rounds
1 head broccoli, cut into
   1 cm (½ inch) pieces
1.5 litres (6 cups) vegetable or chicken
   stock
150 g (5½ oz) green beans, trimmed
   and cut into 1 cm (½ inch) pieces
155 g (1 cup) green peas
155 g (10 spears) asparagus, end
   trimmed and cut into
   1 cm (½ inch) pieces
80 g (2¾ oz/2 cups) shredded
   silverbeet (Swiss chard) leaves

Pistou
3 garlic cloves, peeled
1 large handful basil
80 ml (2½ fl oz/⅓ cup) olive oil
50 g (1¾ oz/½ cup) grated parmesan
   cheese

Heat the olive oil in a large saucepan, and cook the onion, garlic and celery until golden. Add the zucchini and broccoli, and cook for 5 minutes.

Add the stock and bring to the boil. Simmer for 5 minutes, then add the green beans, peas, asparagus and silverbeet. Simmer for 5 minutes, or until the vegetables are tender. Season well with salt and freshly ground black pepper.

To make the pistou, place the garlic and basil in a mortar and pestle or small food processor and crush together. Slowly add the oil, and blend until a smooth paste. Stir in the parmesan, and season well with salt and freshly ground black pepper.

Ladle the soup into bowls and serve with a dollop of pistou.

Serves 4

Vegetable soup

105 g (3½ oz/½ cup) dried red kidney
  beans or borlotti (cranberry) beans
1 tablespoon olive oil
1 leek, halved lengthways and
  chopped
1 small onion, diced
2 carrots, chopped
2 celery stalks, chopped
1 large zucchini (courgette), chopped
1 tablespoon tomato paste
  (concentrated purée)
1 litre (35 fl oz/4 cups) vegetable stock
400 g (14 oz) pumpkin (winter
  squash), cubed
2 potatoes, cubed
3 tablespoons chopped flat-leaf
  (Italian) parsley

Put the beans in a large bowl, cover
with cold water and soak overnight.
Rinse, then transfer to a saucepan,
cover with cold water and cook for
45 minutes, or until just tender. Drain.

Meanwhile, heat the oil in a large
saucepan. Add the leek and onion
and cook over medium heat for
2–3 minutes without browning, or
until they start to soften. Add the
carrot, celery and zucchini and cook
for 3–4 minutes. Add the tomato paste
and stir for a further 1 minute. Pour in
the stock and 1.25 litres (44 fl oz/
5 cups) water and bring to the boil.
Reduce the heat to low and leave to
simmer for 20 minutes.

Add the pumpkin, potato, parsley
and red kidney beans and simmer
for a further 20 minutes, or until the
vegetables are tender and the beans
are cooked. Season to taste. Serve
immediately with crusty wholemeal
(whole-wheat) or wholegrain bread.

Serves 6

Hint: To save time, use a 420 g (15 oz)
tinned red kidney beans. Rinse and
drain well before use.

Cream of asparagus soup

1 kg (2 lb 4 oz) asparagus spears
30 g (1 oz) butter
1 onion, finely chopped
1 litre (35 fl oz/4 cups) vegetable stock
1 small handful basil leaves, chopped
1 teaspoon celery salt
250 ml (9 fl oz/1 cup) pouring
    (whipping) cream

Break off the woody ends from the asparagus (hold both ends of the spear and bend it gently—the woody end will snap off and can be thrown away) and trim off the tips. Blanch the tips in boiling water for 1–2 minutes, refresh in cold water and set aside. Chop the asparagus stems into large pieces.

Melt the butter in a large saucepan and cook the onion for 3–4 minutes over low–medium heat, or until soft and golden. Add the chopped asparagus stems and cook for 1–2 minutes, stirring continuously.

Add the stock, basil and celery salt. Bring to the boil, reduce the heat and simmer, covered, for 30 minutes.

Check that the asparagus is well cooked and soft. If not, simmer for a further 10 minutes. Set aside and allow to cool slightly.

Pour into a food processor and process in batches until smooth. Then sieve into a clean saucepan. Return to the heat, pour in the cream and gently reheat. Do not allow the soup to boil. Season to taste with salt and white pepper. Add the asparagus tips and serve immediately.

Serves 4–6

Caramelised onion and parsnip soup

30 g (1 oz) butter
3 large onions, halved and thinly sliced
2 tablespoons firmly packed soft
  brown sugar
250 ml (9 fl oz/1 cup) dry white wine
3 large parsnips, peeled, chopped
1.25 litres (44 fl oz/5 cups) vegetable
  stock
60 ml (2 fl oz/¼ cup) pouring
  (whipping) cream
fresh thyme leaves, to garnish

Melt the butter in a large saucepan. Add the onion and sugar, and cook over low heat for 10 minutes. Add the wine and parsnip, and simmer, covered, for 20 minutes, or until onion and parsnip are golden and tender.

Pour in the stock, bring to the boil, then reduce the heat and simmer, covered, for 10 minutes. Cool slightly, then place in a blender or food processor and blend in batches until smooth. Season with salt and freshly ground black pepper. Drizzle with a little cream and sprinkle fresh thyme leaves over the top. Serve with toasted crusty bread slices.

Serves 4

Carrot and ginger soup

750 ml (26 fl oz/3 cups) vegetable
  stock
1 tablespoon oil
1 onion, chopped
1 tablespoon grated fresh ginger
1 kg (2 lb 4 oz) carrots, chopped
2 tablespoons chopped coriander
  (cilantro) leaves

Place the stock in a saucepan and
bring to the boil. Heat the oil in a large
heavy-based saucepan, add the onion
and ginger and cook for 2 minutes, or
until the onion has softened.

Add the stock and carrots. Bring to
the boil, then reduce the heat and
simmer for 10–15 minutes, or until
the carrot is cooked and tender.

Allow the liquid to cool slightly, then
place in a blender or food processor
and process in batches until smooth.
Return to the pan and add a little
more stock or water to thin the soup
to your preferred consistency.

Stir in the coriander and season to
taste. Heat gently before serving.

Serves 4

Watercress soup

30 g (1 oz) butter
1 onion, finely chopped
250 g (9 oz) potatoes, diced
625 ml (21½ fl oz/2½ cups) chicken
   stock
1 kg (2 lb 4 oz) watercress, trimmed
   and chopped
125 ml (4 fl oz/½ cup) pouring
   (whipping) cream
125 ml (4 fl oz/½ cup) milk
freshly grated nutmeg
2 tablespoons snipped chives

Melt the butter in a large saucepan and add the onion. Cover the pan and cook over low heat until the onion is softened but not brown. Add the potato and chicken stock and simmer for 12 minutes, or until the potato is tender. Add the watercress and cook for 1 minute.

Remove from heat and leave soup to cool a little before pouring into a blender or food processor. Blend until smooth and return to the cleaned saucepan.

Bring the soup gently back to the boil and stir in the cream and milk. Season with nutmeg, salt and freshly ground black pepper and reheat without boiling. Serve garnished with chives.

Serves 4

Spicy parsnip soup

1.25 litres (44 fl oz/5 cups) vegetable
  or chicken stock
30 g (1 oz) butter
1 white onion, cut into quarters and
  finely sliced
1 leek, finely sliced
500 g (1 lb 2 oz) parsnips, peeled and
  finely sliced
1 tablespoon curry powder
1 teaspoon ground cumin
315 ml (1¼ cups) pouring (whipping)
  cream
10 g (⅓ cup) coriander (cilantro)
  leaves

Bring the stock to the boil in a
saucepan and keep at a low simmer.

Place the butter in a large saucepan
and melt over medium heat. Add the
onion, leek and parsnip and cook,
covered, for 5 minutes. Add the curry
powder and cumin and cook for
1 minute. Stir in the stock and cook,
covered, over medium heat for about
10 minutes, or until tender.

Allow the soup to cool slightly, then
transfer to a blender or food processor
and blend in batches until smooth.
Return to the pan. Stir in the cream
and warm through over low heat.
Season to taste with salt and cracked
black pepper and scatter with
coriander leaves.

Serves 6

Note: This soup is also delicious
without the cream.

Green curry vegetable soup

2 teaspoons peanut oil
1 tablespoon green curry paste
3 makrut (kaffir) lime leaves
1.25 litres (44 fl oz/5 cups) vegetable
  or chicken stock
670 ml (23 fl oz/2²/₃ cups) coconut
  milk
600 g (1 lb 5 oz) butternut pumpkin
  (squash), cut into 1.5 cm (⁵/₈ inch)
  cubes
250 g (9 oz) yellow baby (pattypan)
  squash, sliced
115 g (4 oz) fresh baby corn spears,
  halved lengthways
2 tablespoons mushroom soy sauce
2 tablespoons lime juice
1 teaspoon sugar
1¹/₂ tablespoons Vietnamese mint,
  finely chopped

Heat the oil in a large saucepan and add the curry paste and lime leaves. Cook, stirring, over medium heat for 1 minute, or until the mixture is fragrant. Bring the stock to the boil in a separate saucepan.

Gradually add the stock and coconut milk to the curry mixture and bring to the boil. Add the pumpkin, squash and corn, and simmer over low heat for 12 minutes, or until the pumpkin is tender.

Add the soy sauce and lime juice, and season to taste with sugar, salt and freshly ground black pepper. Sprinkle with the mint before serving.

Serves 6

Tuscan-style ribollita

60 ml (2 fl oz/¼ cup) extra virgin
    olive oil
1 onion, cut into 1 cm (½ inch) chunks
1 carrot, cut into 1 cm (½ inch) chunks
40 g (1½ oz) pancetta, chopped
2 garlic cloves, crushed
¼ small green cabbage (about
    250 g/9 oz), core and tough outer
    leaves discarded, leaves roughly
    chopped
1 tablespoon tomato paste
    (concentrated purée)
400 g (14 oz) tinned chopped
    tomatoes
400 g (14 oz/½ bunch) silverbeet
    (Swiss chard), stems removed,
    leaves washed, dried and thinly
    sliced
400 g (14 oz) tinned cannellini beans,
    rinsed and drained
750 ml (26 fl oz/3 cups) chicken stock
1 bay leaf
3 cm (1¼ inch) piece of parmesan
    cheese rind
200 g (7 oz) piece of day-old rustic-
    style bread, torn into 1 cm (½ inch)
    chunks (about 2 cups)
65 g (2½ oz/⅔ cup) shaved parmesan
    cheese

Heat the oil in a large heavy-based saucepan over medium heat. Add the onion, carrot, pancetta, garlic and cabbage and sauté for 7 minutes, or until the vegetables are lightly golden.

Stir in the tomato paste, tomatoes and silverbeet, then the beans, stock, bay leaf and parmesan rind. Bring the soup just to a simmer, then cook over low heat for 30 minutes, or until the vegetables are very tender.

Stir in the bread chunks, then cover and leave for 2–3 minutes, or until the bread is soft.

Divide the soup among warm deep bowls. Scatter the shaved parmesan over the soup and serve immediately.

Serves 6

Split pea and vegetable soup

1 tablespoon peanut or vegetable oil
1 onion, chopped
2 garlic cloves, chopped
1½ teaspoons chopped fresh ginger
1½ tablespoons curry paste
100 g (3½ oz) yellow split peas, rinsed
  and drained
1 large zucchini (courgette), peeled
  and chopped
1 large carrot, roughly chopped
170 g (6 oz) button mushrooms,
  roughly chopped
1 celery stalk, roughly chopped
1 litre (35 fl oz/4 cups) vegetable stock
125 ml (4 fl oz/½ cup) pouring
  (whipping) cream

Heat the oil in a saucepan, add the onion and cook over low heat for 5 minutes, or until soft. Add the garlic, ginger and curry paste and cook over medium heat for 2 minutes. Stir in the split peas until well coated with paste, then add the zucchini, carrot, mushroom and celery and cook for 2 minutes.

Add the stock, bring to the boil, then reduce the heat and simmer, partly covered, for 1 hour. Remove from the heat and allow to cool slightly.

Transfer the soup to a blender or food processor and process in batches until smooth. Return to the pan, stir in the cream and gently heat until warmed through. Delicious served with naan bread.

Serves 4

Cream of fennel and leek soup

30 g (1 oz) butter
2 large fennel bulbs, thinly sliced
2 leeks, thinly sliced
1 litre (35 fl oz/4 cups) hot vegetable
  or chicken stock
2 rosemary sprigs
⅛ teaspoon ground nutmeg
80 g (2¾ oz/⅓ cup) sour cream
25 g (1 oz/¼ cup) finely grated
  parmesan cheese
1 tablespoon oil
1 leek, extra, cut in half lengthways,
  and cut into 4 cm (1½ inch) lengths
grated parmesan cheese, extra, to
  garnish
sour cream, extra, to garnish

Heat the butter in a large heavy-based saucepan, add sliced fennel and leek, and cook, covered, over medium heat for 2–3 minutes, stirring occasionally.

Put the hot stock, rosemary sprigs and nutmeg in a saucepan and bring to the boil. Simmer over low heat for about 15 minutes, then remove the rosemary sprigs and add the fennel and leek mixture to the pan.

Allow the soup to cool slightly, then transfer to a blender or food processor and blend in batches until smooth. Return to the pan, and stir in the sour cream and parmesan. Reheat over medium heat until hot. Season to taste with salt and cracked black pepper and keep warm.

Heat the oil in a frying pan and cook the extra leek for 2–3 minutes, or until soft but not browned.

Spoon the soup into six warm soup bowls and top with the fried leek. Garnish with the extra parmesan and sour cream and serve immediately.

Serves 6

Fresh mushroom, shallot and sour cream soup

2 tablespoons butter
100 g (3½ oz/about 4) French shallots, roughly chopped
3 garlic cloves, crushed
30 g (1 oz/1 cup) firmly packed flat-leaf (Italian) parsley
315 ml (1¼ cups) vegetable or chicken stock
315 ml (1¼ cups) milk
600 g (1 lb 5 oz) button mushrooms
¼ teaspoon ground nutmeg
¼ teaspoon cayenne pepper
150 g (5½ oz) light sour cream
cayenne pepper, to garnish

Melt the butter in a large heavy-based saucepan and add the shallots, garlic and parsley. Cook over medium heat for 2–3 minutes. Put the stock and milk in a separate saucepan and bring to the boil.

Gently wipe the mushrooms, then chop and add to the shallot mixture. Season with salt and freshly ground black pepper, and stir in the nutmeg and cayenne pepper. Cook, stirring, for 1 minute. Add the stock and milk, bring to the boil, then reduce the heat and simmer for 5 minutes. Allow the soup to cool slightly, then transfer to a blender or food processor and blend until smooth. Return to the pan.

Stir in the sour cream, adjust the seasoning and reheat gently. Serve sprinkled with cayenne pepper.

Serves 4

Note: For an ideal garnish, fry diced button mushrooms in a little butter until golden. This can be prepared during the soup's final simmering.

Vegetable and lentil soup with spiced yoghurt

2 tablespoons olive oil
1 small leek, white part only, chopped
2 garlic cloves, crushed
2 teaspoons curry powder
1 teaspoon ground cumin
1 teaspoon garam masala
1 litre (35 fl oz/4 cups) vegetable stock
1 bay leaf
185 g (6½ oz/1 cup) brown lentils
450 g (1 lb) butternut pumpkin
    (squash), peeled and cut into
    1 cm (½ inch) cubes
2 zucchini (courgettes), cut in half
    lengthways and sliced
400 g (14 oz) tinned chopped
    tomatoes
200 g (7 oz) broccoli, cut into small
    florets
1 small carrot, diced
80 g (2¾ oz/½ cup) peas
1 tablespoon chopped mint

Spiced yoghurt
250 g (9 oz/1 cup) thick plain yoghurt
1 tablespoon chopped coriander
    (cilantro) leaves
1 garlic clove, crushed
3 dashes Tabasco sauce

Heat the oil in a saucepan over medium heat. Add the leek and garlic and cook for 4–5 minutes, or until soft and lightly golden. Add the curry powder, cumin and garam masala and cook for 1 minute, or until fragrant.

Add the stock, bay leaf, lentils and pumpkin. Bring to the boil, then reduce the heat to low and simmer for 10–15 minutes, or until the lentils are tender. Season well.

Add the zucchini, tomatoes, broccoli, carrot and 500 ml (17 fl oz/2 cups) water and simmer for 10 minutes, or until the vegetables are tender. Add the peas and simmer for 2–3 minutes.

To make the spiced yoghurt, place the yoghurt, coriander, garlic and Tabasco in a small bowl and stir until combined.

Dollop a spoonful of the yoghurt on each serving of soup and garnish with the chopped mint.

Serves 6

Pumpkin, lentil and tomato soup with cheesy toasts

2 tablespoons olive oil
1 kg (2 lb 4 oz) pumpkin (winter
    squash), peeled, seeded and cut
    into 2 cm (3/4 inch) chunks
2 carrots, finely chopped
2 onions, finely chopped
1 large celery stalk, finely chopped
3 garlic cloves, crushed
1.5 litres (52 fl oz/6 cups) vegetable or
    chicken stock
125 g (4½ oz/½ cup) red lentils
400 g (14 oz) tinned chopped
    tomatoes
1 tablespoon finely chopped parsley
    or coriander (cilantro) leaves

Cheesy toasts
8 slices of ciabatta or other rustic
    bread, cut about 2 cm (3/4 inch) thick
85 g (3 oz/2/3 cup) finely grated
    cheddar cheese

Heat the oil in a large saucepan over medium heat. Add the vegetables and garlic and sauté for 5 minutes, or until softened but not browned.

Stir in the stock, lentils and tomatoes. Bring to the boil, then reduce the heat to medium–low and simmer for 20 minutes, or until the lentils are tender. Season well with sea salt and freshly ground black pepper.

Meanwhile, make the cheesy toasts. Heat the grill (broiler) to medium, then place the bread slices on a baking tray and toast under the grill on one side. Turn the toasts over and scatter with the grated cheese. Grill for 3–4 minutes, or until the cheese has melted and is golden brown.

Ladle the soup into bowls or cups, sprinkle with parsley and serve with the hot cheesy toasts.

Serves 4

Potato and rocket soup

1.5 litres (52 fl oz/6 cups) vegetable or
  chicken stock
1.25 kg (2 lb 12 oz) desiree potatoes,
  chopped into small pieces
2 large garlic cloves, peeled, left whole
250 g (9 oz) rocket (arugula)
1 tablespoon extra virgin olive oil
extra rocket (arugula) leaves, to
  garnish (optional)
50 g (1¾ oz/½ cup) shaved parmesan
  cheese

Place the stock in a large heavy-based
saucepan and bring to the boil. Add
the potato and garlic and simmer over
medium heat for 15 minutes, or until
the potato is tender to the point of
a sharp knife. Add the rocket and
simmer for a further 2 minutes. Stir in
the olive oil.

Allow the mixture to cool slightly, then
transfer to a blender or food processor
and blend in batches until smooth.
Return the mixture to the pan and stir
over medium heat until hot. Season to
taste with salt and cracked black
pepper and serve in warmed bowls.
Garnish with the rocket leaves and
shaved parmesan before serving.

Serves 6

Curried sweet potato soup

1 tablespoon oil
1 large onion, chopped
2 garlic cloves, crushed
3 teaspoons curry powder
1.25 kg (2 lb 12 oz) orange sweet
    potato, peeled and cubed
1 litre (35 fl oz/4 cups) chicken stock
1 large apple, peeled, cored and
    grated
125 ml (4 fl oz/$\frac{1}{2}$ cup) light coconut
    milk

Heat the oil in a large saucepan over medium heat and cook the onion for 10 minutes, stirring occasionally, until very soft. Add the garlic and curry powder and cook for a further 1 minute.

Add the sweet potato, stock and apple. Bring to the boil, reduce the heat and simmer, partially covered, for 30 minutes, until very soft.

Cool the soup a little before processing in batches until smooth. Return to the pan, stir in the coconut milk and reheat gently without boiling. Serve with warm pitta bread.

Serves 6

Storage time: Can be kept in the fridge for 1 day without the coconut milk: add this when you reheat.

Zucchini pesto soup

1 tablespoon olive oil
1 large onion, finely chopped
2 garlic cloves, crushed
750 ml (26 fl oz/3 cups) vegetable or
  chicken stock
750 g (1 lb 10 oz) zucchini
  (courgettes), thinly sliced
60 ml (2 fl oz/¼ cup) pouring
  (whipping) cream
toasted ciabatta bread, to serve

Pesto
2 large handfuls basil
25 g (1 oz/¼ cup) finely grated
  parmesan cheese
2 tablespoons pine nuts, toasted
2 tablespoons extra virgin olive oil

Heat the oil in a large heavy-based saucepan. Add the onion and garlic and cook over medium heat for 5 minutes, or until the onion is soft.

Bring the stock to the boil in a separate saucepan. Add the zucchini and hot stock to the onion mixture. Bring to the boil, then reduce the heat, cover and simmer for about 10 minutes, or until the zucchini is very soft.

To make the pesto, process the basil, parmesan and pine nuts in a food processor for 20 seconds, or until finely chopped. Gradually add the olive oil and process until smooth. Spoon into a small bowl.

Transfer the zucchini mixture to a blender or food processor and blend in batches until smooth. Return the mixture to the pan, stir in the cream and 2 tablespoons of the pesto, and reheat over medium heat until hot. Season with salt and freshly ground black pepper and serve with toasted ciabatta bread. Serve the remaining pesto in a bowl for diners to help themselves, or cover with olive oil and store in the refrigerator for up to 1 week.

Serves 4

Minestrone with pesto

125 g (4½ oz) dried borlotti (cranberry) beans
1 large onion, roughly chopped
2 garlic cloves
3 tablespoons chopped parsley
60 g (2¼ oz) pancetta, chopped
3 tablespoons olive oil
1 celery stalk, halved lengthways, then cut into 1 cm (½ inch) slices
1 carrot, halved lengthways, then cut into 1 cm (½ inch) slices
1 all-purpose potato, diced
2 teaspoons tomato paste (concentrated purée)
400 g (14 oz) tinned chopped tomatoes
6 basil leaves, roughly torn
2 litres (70 fl oz/8 cups) chicken or vegetable stock
2 thin zucchini (courgettes), cut into thick slices
120 g (4¼ oz/¾ cup) shelled fresh peas
60 g (2¼ oz/½ cup) green beans, cut into short lengths
90 g (3¼ oz) silverbeet (Swiss chard) leaves, shredded
75 g (2½ oz) ditalini or other small pasta

Pesto
1 very large handful basil leaves
1 tablespoon lightly toasted pine nuts
2 garlic cloves
100 ml (3½ fl oz) olive oil
30 g (1 oz) grated parmesan cheese

Put the borlotti beans in a large bowl, cover with water and soak overnight. Drain and rinse under cold water.

Put the onion, garlic, parsley and pancetta in a food processor and process until fine. Heat the oil in a saucepan, add the pancetta mixture and cook over low heat, stirring occasionally, for 8–10 minutes.

Add the celery, carrot and potato, and cook for 5 minutes, then stir in the tomato paste, tomato, basil and borlotti beans. Season with freshly ground black pepper. Add the stock and bring slowly to the boil. Cover and simmer, stirring occasionally, for 1 hour 30 minutes.

Season and add the zucchini, peas, green beans, silverbeet and pasta. Simmer for 8–10 minutes, or until the vegetables and pasta are *al dente*.

To make the pesto, combine the basil, pine nuts and garlic with a pinch of salt in a food processor. Process until finely chopped. With the motor running, slowly add the olive oil. Transfer to a bowl and stir in the parmesan and freshly ground black pepper to taste. Serve the soup in bowls with the pesto on top.

Serves 6

Ratatouille and pasta soup

1 eggplant (aubergine), chopped
1 tablespoon olive oil
1 large onion, chopped
1 large red capsicum (pepper),
   chopped
1 large green capsicum (pepper),
   chopped
2 garlic cloves, crushed
3 zucchini (courgettes), sliced
800 g (1 lb 12 oz) tinned chopped
   tomatoes
1 teaspoon dried oregano leaves
1/2 teaspoon dried thyme leaves
1 litre (35 fl oz/4 cups) vegetable stock
45 g (1 1/2 oz) pasta spirals
parmesan cheese, to serve

Spread the eggplant out in a colander
and sprinkle generously with salt.
Leave for 20 minutes; rinse and pat
dry with paper towels.

Heat the oil in a large heavy-based
saucepan and cook the onion for
10 minutes, or until soft and lightly
golden. Add the capsicum, garlic,
zucchini and eggplant and cook for
5 minutes.

Add the tomato, herbs and stock to
the pan. Bring to the boil, then reduce
the heat and simmer for 10 minutes,
or until the vegetables are tender. Add
the pasta and cook for 15 minutes,
until *al dente*. Serve with parmesan
cheese and bread.

Serves 6

Storage: This soup will keep for up to
2 days in the refrigerator.

Prawn, potato and corn chowder

600 g raw medium prawns (shrimp)
3 corn cobs, husks removed
1 tablespoon olive oil
2 leeks, white part only, finely chopped
2 garlic cloves, crushed
650 g potatoes, cut into 1.5 cm cubes
750 ml (26 fl oz/3 cups) fish or
  chicken stock
375 ml (13 fl oz/1½ cups) milk
250 ml (9 fl oz/1 cup) pouring
  (whipping) cream
pinch of cayenne pepper
3 tablespoons finely chopped fresh
  flat-leaf (Italian) parsley

Peel and devein the prawns, then chop them into 1.5 cm ($^5/_8$ inch) pieces.

Cut the kernels from the corn cobs. Heat the oil in a large saucepan and add the leek. Cook over medium–low heat for about 5 minutes, or until soft and lightly golden. Add the garlic and cook for 30 seconds, then add the corn, potato, stock and milk.

Bring to the boil, then reduce the heat and simmer, partially covered, for about 20 minutes, or until the potato is soft but still holds its shape (it will break down slightly). Remove the lid and simmer for a further 10 minutes to allow the soup to thicken. Reduce the heat to low. Allow the soup to cool slightly, then put 500 ml (17 fl oz/ 2 cups) of the soup in a blender and blend until very smooth.

Return the blended soup to the saucepan and add the prawns. Increase the heat to medium and simmer for 2 minutes, or until the prawns are pink and cooked through. Stir in the cream, cayenne pepper and 2 tablespoons of the parsley. Season to taste with salt, then serve garnished with the remaining parsley.

Serves 4–6

Pea and rocket soup

1 tablespoon olive oil
1 red onion, finely chopped
700 g (1 lb 9 oz) frozen peas
100 g (3½ oz) rocket (arugula) leaves
750 ml (26 fl oz/3 cups) hot vegetable
  stock
shaved parmesan cheese, to garnish
rocket leaves, extra, to garnish

Heat the oil in a large saucepan over medium heat. Add the onion and cook for 5 minutes, or until soft. Add the peas and rocket, and cook for a further 2 minutes. Add the stock and 250 ml (9 fl oz/1 cup) water, bring to the boil, then reduce the heat and simmer for 20 minutes.

Cool slightly then place in a food processor or blender in batches and process until almost smooth. Return to the cleaned saucepan and heat through. Serve garnished with shaved parmesan and the extra rocket.

Serves 4

Vegetable ramen

375 g fresh ramen noodles
1 tablespoon oil
1 tablespoon finely chopped fresh
  ginger
2 garlic cloves, crushed
150 g (5½ oz) oyster mushrooms,
  halved
1 small zucchini (courgette), sliced into
  thin rounds
1 leek, white and light green part,
  halved lengthways and thinly sliced
100 g (3½ oz) snow peas (mangetout),
  halved diagonally
100 g (3½ oz) fried tofu puffs, cut into
  matchsticks
1.25 litres (44 fl oz/5 cups) vegetable
  stock
1½ tablespoons white miso paste
2 tablespoons light soy sauce
1 tablespoon mirin
90 g (3¼ oz/1 cup) bean sprouts
1 teaspoon sesame oil
4 spring onions, thinly sliced
100 g (3½ oz) enoki mushrooms

Bring a large saucepan of lightly salted water to the boil. Add the noodles and cook, stirring to prevent sticking, for 4 minutes, or until just tender. Drain and rinse under cold running water.

Heat the oil in a large saucepan over medium heat, add the ginger, crushed garlic, oyster mushrooms, zucchini, leek, snow peas and tofu puffs, and stir-fry for 2 minutes. Add the stock and 300 ml (1½ fl oz) water and bring to the boil, then reduce the heat and simmer. Stir in the miso, soy sauce and mirin until heated through. Do not boil. Stir in the bean sprouts and sesame oil.

Place the noodles in the bottom of six serving bowls, then pour in the soup. Garnish with the spring onion and enoki mushrooms.

Serves 6

Chicken and pumpkin laksa

Paste

2 bird's eye chillies, seeded and
  roughly chopped
2 stems lemongrass, white part only,
  roughly chopped
4 red Asian shallots, peeled
1 tablespoon roughly chopped fresh
  ginger
1 teaspoon ground turmeric
3 candlenuts, optional

110 g (3¾ oz) dried rice noodle sticks
1 tablespoon peanut oil
250 g (9 oz) butternut pumpkin
  (squash), cut into 2 cm (¾ inch)
  chunks
800 ml (28 fl oz) coconut milk
600 g boneless, skinless chicken
  breasts, cut into cubes
2 tablespoons lime juice
1 tablespoon fish sauce
90 g (3¼ oz) bean sprouts
1 medium handful torn fresh basil
1 medium handful torn fresh mint
50 g (1¾ oz/½ cup) unsalted peanuts,
  toasted and chopped
1 lime, cut into quarters

Place all the paste ingredients in a
food processor with 1 tablespoon
water and blend until smooth.

Soak the noodles in boiling water
for 15–20 minutes. Drain.

Meanwhile, heat the oil in a wok
and swirl to coat. Add the paste
and stir over low heat for 5 minutes,
or until aromatic. Add the pumpkin
and coconut milk and simmer for
10 minutes. Add the chicken and
simmer for 20 minutes. Stir in the
lime juice and fish sauce.

Divide the noodles among four deep
serving bowls, then ladle the soup
over them. Garnish with the bean
sprouts, basil, mint, peanuts and lime.

Serves 4

Caribbean fish soup

2 tomatoes
2 tablespoons oil
4 French shallots, finely chopped
2 celery stalks, chopped
1 large red capsicum (pepper), chopped
1 Scotch bonnet chilli, deseeded and finely chopped (see Note)
1/2 teaspoon ground allspice
1/2 teaspoon freshly grated nutmeg
875 ml (30 fl oz/3½ cups) fish stock
275 g (9¾ oz) orange sweet potato, peeled and cut into cubes
60 ml (2 fl oz/¼ cup) lime juice
500 g (1 lb 2 oz) skinless sea bream fillets, cut into chunks

Fish substitution
sea bass, cod

Score a cross in the base of each tomato. Soak in boiling water for 30 seconds, then plunge into cold water. Drain and peel the skin away from the cross. Chop the tomatoes, discarding the cores, and reserving any juices.

Heat the oil in a large saucepan, then add the shallots, celery, capsicum, chilli, allspice and nutmeg. Cook for 4–5 minutes, or until the vegetables have softened, stirring now and then. Tip in the chopped tomatoes (including their juices) and stock and bring to the boil. Reduce the heat to medium and add the cubes of sweet potato. Season to taste with salt and freshly ground black pepper and cook for about 15 minutes, or until the sweet potato is tender.

Add the lime juice and chunks of fish to the saucepan and poach gently for 4–5 minutes, or until the fish is cooked through. Season to taste, then serve with lots of crusty bread.

Serves 6

Note: Scotch bonnet chillies looks like a mini capsicum (pepper) and can be green, red or orange. They are extremely hot but have a good, slightly acidic flavour.

Grilled Italian sausage and vegetable soup

500 g (1 lb 2 oz) Italian pork sausages
200 g (7 oz) piece speck (see Note)
1 tablespoon olive oil
1 large onion, chopped
3 garlic cloves, crushed
1 celery stalk, cut in half and sliced
1 large carrot, cut into 1 cm (½ inch) cubes
bouquet garni (1 parsley sprig, 1 oregano sprig, 2 bay leaves)
1 small red chilli, halved lengthways
400 g (14 oz) tinned chopped tomatoes
1.75 litres (59 fl oz/7 cups) chicken stock
300 g (10½ oz) brussels sprouts, cut in half from top to base
300 g (10½ oz) green beans, cut into 3 cm (1¼ inch) lengths
300 g (10½ oz) shelled broad beans, fresh or frozen
2 tablespoons chopped flat-leaf (Italian) parsley

Grill (broil) the sausages under a hot grill (broiler) for 8–10 minutes, turning occasionally, or until brown. Remove and cut into 3 cm (1¼ inch) lengths. Trim and reserve the fat from the speck, then dice the speck.

Heat the oil in a large saucepan over medium heat. Add the speck and reserved speck fat and cook for 2–3 minutes, or until golden. Add the onion, garlic, celery and carrot, reduce the heat to low and cook for 6–8 minutes, or until softened. Discard the remains of the speck fat.

Stir in the sausages, bouquet garni, chilli and chopped tomato and cook for 5 minutes. Add the stock, bring to the boil, then reduce the heat and simmer for 1 hour. Add the brussels sprouts, green beans and broad beans and simmer for 30 minutes. Discard the bouquet garni, then stir in the parsley. Season to taste. Divide among four bowls and serve.

Serves 4

Note: Speck is cured smoked ham or pork belly. It has a strong taste and is usually cut into small pieces and used as a flavour base.

Beef borscht

2 tablespoons olive oil
500 g (1 lb 2 oz) gravy beef or oyster
 blade, trimmed and cut into 2.5 cm
 (1 inch) chunks
2 onions, finely chopped
1 garlic clove, finely chopped
1 celery stalk, finely chopped
2 beetroot (beets), scrubbed, trimmed
 and cut in half
2 potatoes (500 g/1 lb 2 oz in total),
 peeled and cut into 1 cm (1/2 inch)
 chunks
2 carrots, coarsely grated
1/4 savoy cabbage (about 300 g/
 101/2 oz), core removed, then finely
 shredded
1 tablespoon chopped flat-leaf (Italian)
 parsley
1 bay leaf
1 teaspoon dill seeds
1/2 teaspoon celery seeds
500 ml (17 fl oz/2 cups) beef stock
2 tablespoons lemon juice, or to taste
3 tablespoons chopped dill
125 g (41/2 oz/1/2 cup) sour cream
4 slices dark rye bread, toasted

Heat the olive oil in a large heavy-based saucepan over medium–high heat. Add the beef in batches and cook for 3 minutes, turning often, or until browned. Remove each batch to a plate and set aside.

Add the onion, garlic and celery to the pan and sauté for 5 minutes, or until softened. Stir in the beetroot, potato, carrot and cabbage. Return the beef to the saucepan and add the parsley, bay leaf, dill and celery seeds. Pour in the stock and 1.5 litres (52 fl oz/ 6 cups) water and bring to the boil, then reduce the heat to low and simmer for 30–45 minutes, or until the vegetables and beef are very tender.

Remove and discard the bay leaf. Scoop out the beetroot halves and leave until cool enough to handle, then peel off the skin. Grate the beetroot and stir into the soup. Season to taste with sea salt and freshly ground black pepper, then stir in the lemon juice.

Mix 1 tablespoon of the dill through the sour cream, then spread over the toasted bread slices.

Ladle the soup into warm bowls, garnish with the remaining dill and serve with the toast slices.

Serves 6

Cabbage soup

100 g (3½ oz/½ cup) dried haricot
   beans
125 g (4½ oz) bacon, cubed
40 g (1½ oz) butter
1 carrot, sliced
1 onion, chopped
1 leek, white part only, roughly
   chopped
1 turnip, peeled and chopped
bouquet garni (1 parsley sprig,
   1 oregano sprig, 2 bay leaves)
1.25 litres (44 fl oz/5 cups) chicken
   stock
400 g (14 oz) white cabbage, finely
   shredded

Soak the beans overnight in cold
water. Drain, put in a saucepan and
cover with cold water. Bring to the boil
and simmer for 5 minutes, then drain.
Put the bacon in the same saucepan,
cover with water and simmer for
5 minutes. Drain and pat dry with
paper towels.

Melt the butter in a large heavy-based
saucepan, add the bacon and cook
for 5 minutes, without browning. Add
the beans, carrot, onion, leek and
turnip and cook for 5 minutes. Add
the bouquet garni and chicken stock
and bring to the boil. Cover and
simmer for 30 minutes. Add the
cabbage, uncover and simmer for
30 minutes, or until the beans are
tender. Remove the bouquet garni
before serving and season to taste.

Serves 4

Oxtail soup with stout and vegetables

2 kg (4 lb 8 oz) oxtails, trimmed
2 tablespoons vegetable oil
2 onions, finely chopped
1 leek, finely chopped
2 carrots, diced
1 celery stalk, diced
2 garlic cloves, crushed
2 bay leaves
2 tablespoons tomato paste
    (concentrated purée)
1 thyme sprig
2 flat-leaf (Italian) parsley sprigs
3.5 litres (118½ fl oz/14 cups) chicken
    stock
375 ml (13 fl oz/1½ cups) stout
2 tomatoes, seeded and diced
100 g (3½ oz) cauliflower florets
100 g (3½ oz) green beans
100 g (3½ oz) broccoli florets
100 g (3½ oz/6 spears) asparagus,
    cut into 3 cm (1¼ inch) lengths

Preheat the oven to 200°C (400°F/ Gas 6). Place the oxtails in a baking tray and bake for 1 hour, turning occasionally, or until dark golden. Leave to cool.

Heat the oil in a large saucepan over medium heat and cook the onion, leek, carrot and celery for 3–4 minutes, or until soft. Stir in the garlic, bay leaves and tomato paste, then add the oxtails, thyme and parsley.

Add the stock and bring to the boil over high heat. Reduce the heat and simmer for 3 hours, or until the oxtails are tender and the meat falls off the bone. Skim off any scum that rises to the surface. Remove the oxtails and cool slightly.

Take the meat off the bones and discard any fat or sinew. Roughly chop and add to the soup with the stout, tomato and 500 ml (17 fl oz/ 2 cups) water. Add the vegetables and simmer for 5 minutes, or until the vegetables are tender. Season.

Serves 4

Tomato and capsicum soup with polenta and olive sticks

2 tablespoons vegetable oil
2 tablespoons olive oil
2 red onions, finely chopped
2 garlic cloves, crushed
1 tablespoon ground cumin
¼ teaspoon ground cayenne pepper
2 teaspoons paprika
2 red capsicums (peppers), diced
90 g (3¼ oz/⅓ cup) tomato paste
   (concentrated purée)
250 ml (9 fl oz/1 cup) dry white wine
2 x 400 g (14 oz) tinned chopped
   tomatoes
2 long red chillies, seeded and
   chopped
500 ml (17 fl oz/2 cups) chicken or
   vegetable stock
3 tablespoons chopped flat-leaf
   (Italian) parsley
4 tablespoons chopped coriander
   (cilantro) leaves

Polenta and olive sticks
500 ml (17 fl oz/2 cups) chicken or
   vegetable stock
185 g (6½ oz/1¼ cups) coarse
   polenta (cornmeal)
100 g (3½ oz) pitted Kalamata olives,
   chopped
125 ml (4 fl oz/½ cup) olive oil, to
   deep-fry

Heat the oils in a large saucepan over medium heat and cook the onion and garlic for 2–3 minutes, or until soft.

Reduce the heat to low, add the spices and cook for 1–2 minutes. Add the capsicum and cook for 5 minutes. Stir in the tomato paste and wine, simmer for 2 minutes, or until reduced slightly. Add the tomato, chilli, stock and 500 ml (17 fl oz/2 cups) water. Season. Simmer for 20 minutes. Allow the soup to cool slightly, then purée with the herbs.

To make the polenta and olive sticks, grease a 20 x 30 cm (8 x 12 inch) shallow baking tray. Bring the stock and 500 ml (17 fl oz/2 cups) water to the boil in a saucepan. Slowly add the polenta in a fine stream, whisking until smooth. Reduce the heat to low. Cook, stirring constantly, for 15–20 minutes, or until it starts to come away from the side. Stir in the olives, then spoon into the tray, smoothing the surface. Cover and chill for 30 minutes. Cut into sticks.

Heat the oil in a large deep frying pan to 190°C (375°F), or until a cube of bread browns in 10 seconds. Cook the sticks in batches on each side for 1–2 minutes, or until crisp. Drain well, and serve with the soup.

Serves 4–6

Chicken and vegetable soup

1.5 kg (3 lb 5 oz) chicken
1 onion
2 large leeks, halved lengthwise and
  well washed
3 large celery stalks
5 black peppercorns
1 bay leaf
2 large carrots, peeled and diced
1 large swede (rutabaga), peeled and
  diced
2 large tomatoes, peeled, seeded and
  finely chopped
165 g (5¾ oz/¾ cup) barley
1 tablespoon tomato paste
  (concentrated purée)
2 tablespoons finely chopped flat-leaf
  (Italian) parsley

Put the chicken, onion, 1 leek, 1 celery stalk, halved, the peppercorns and bay leaf in a large saucepan and add enough water to cover. Bring to the boil, then reduce the heat and simmer for 1½ hours, skimming any impurities that rise to the surface.

Strain the stock through a fine sieve and return to the cleaned saucepan. Discard the onion, leek, celery, peppercorns and bay leaf, and set the chicken aside. When it is cool enough to handle, discard the fat and bones, then shred the flesh, cover and chill.

Allow the stock to cool, then refrigerate overnight. Skim the fat from the surface, place the stock in a large saucepan and bring to the boil. Dice the remaining leek and celery and add to the soup with the carrot, swede, tomato, barley and tomato paste. Simmer for 45–50 minutes, or until the vegetables are cooked and the barley is tender. Stir in the parsley and shredded chicken. Simmer until warmed through and season.

Serves 4–6

Winter lamb shank soup

1 tablespoon olive oil
1.25 kg (2 lb 12 oz) lamb shanks
2 onions, chopped
4 garlic cloves, chopped
250 ml (9 fl oz/1 cup) red wine
2 bay leaves
1 tablespoon chopped rosemary
2.5 litres (84½ fl oz/10 cups) beef
  stock
425 g (15 oz) tinned crushed
  tomatoes
165 g (5¾oz/¾ cup) pearl barley,
  rinsed and drained
1 large carrot, diced
1 potato, diced
1 turnip, diced
1 parsnip, diced
2 tablespoons redcurrant jelly
  (optional)

Heat the oil in a large saucepan over high heat. Cook the lamb shanks for 2–3 minutes, or until brown. Remove.

Add the onion to the pan and cook over low heat for 8 minutes, or until soft. Add the garlic and cook for 30 seconds, then add the wine and simmer for 5 minutes.

Add the shanks, bay leaves, half the rosemary and 1.5 litres (52 fl oz/ 6 cups) of the stock to the pan. Season. Bring to the boil over high heat. Reduce the heat and simmer, covered, for 2 hours, or until the meat falls off the bone. Remove the shanks and cool slightly.

Take the meat off the bone and roughly chop. Add to the broth with the tomato, barley, the remaining rosemary and stock and simmer for 30 minutes. Add the vegetables and cook for 1 hour, or until the barley is tender. Remove the bay leaves, then stir in the redcurrant jelly.

Serves 4

Cauliflower and almond soup with hot cheese rolls

80 g (2¾ oz/½ cup) blanched
  almonds
1 tablespoon olive oil
1 large leek (white part only), chopped
2 garlic cloves, crushed
1 kg (2 lb 4 oz) cauliflower, cut into
  small florets
2 desiree potatoes, (about 370 g/
  13 oz), cut into 1.5 cm (⅝ inch)
  pieces
1.75 litres (59 fl oz/7 cups) chicken
  stock

Cheese rolls
4 round bread rolls
40 g (1½ oz) softened butter
125 g (4½ oz) cheddar cheese, grated
50 g (1¾ oz) parmesan cheese,
  grated

Preheat oven to 180°C (350°F/Gas 4).
Place the almonds on a baking tray
and toast for 5 minutes, or until golden.

Heat the oil in a large saucepan over
medium heat and cook the leek for
2–3 minutes, or until softened. Add
the garlic and cook for 30 seconds,
then add the cauliflower, potato and
stock. Bring to the boil, then reduce
the heat and simmer for 15 minutes,
or until the vegetables are very tender.
Cool for 5 minutes.

Allow the soup to cool slightly, then
with the almonds in batches in a
blender until smooth. Season to taste
with salt and freshly ground black
pepper. Return to the cleaned pan
and stir over medium heat until heated
through. Serve with the cheese rolls,
if desired.

To make the cheese rolls, split the rolls
and butter both sides. Combine the
grated cheeses and divide evenly
among the rolls. Sandwich together
and wrap in foil. Bake in the oven for
15–20 minutes, or until the cheese
has melted.

Serves 4

Creamy brussels sprout and leek soup

1 tablespoon olive oil
2 rindless bacon slices, chopped
2 garlic cloves, chopped
3 leeks, white part only, sliced
300 g (10½ oz) brussels sprouts, roughly chopped
750 ml (26 fl oz/3 cups) chicken or vegetable stock
185 ml (6 fl oz/¾ cup) pouring (whipping) cream or milk
slices of toasted crusty bread, to serve

Heat the oil in a large saucepan over medium heat. Add chopped bacon and fry for 3 minutes. Add the garlic and leek, cover and fry, stirring often, for a further 5 minutes. Add brussels sprouts, stir to combine, cover and cook, stirring often, for 5 minutes.

Add the stock and season with salt and freshly ground black pepper. Bring to the boil, then reduce heat, cover pan and simmer for 10 minutes, or until vegetables are very tender. Set aside to cool for 10 minutes.

Using an immersion blender fitted with a chopping blade, blend the soup for 25–30 seconds, or until puréed. Stir through the cream or milk and gently reheat the soup. Serve with slices of toasted crusty bread.

Serves 4

Tip: For a vegetarian version of this soup, simply omit the bacon and use vegetable stock rather than chicken stock.

Potato, broccoli and cauliflower soup

500 g (1 lb 2 oz) broccoli
cooking oil spray
2 onions, finely chopped
2 garlic cloves, finely chopped
2 teaspoons ground cumin
1 teaspoon ground coriander
750 g (1 lb 10 oz) potatoes, cubed
2 small chicken stock (bouillon) cubes
375 ml (13 fl oz/1½ cups) skim milk
3 tablespoons finely chopped
   coriander (cilantro)

Cut the broccoli into small pieces. Lightly spray base of a large saucepan with oil and place over medium heat. Add the onion and garlic and 1 tablespoon water. Cover the pan. Cook, stirring occasionally, over low heat for 5 minutes, or until the onion has softened and is lightly golden. Add the ground cumin and coriander and cook for 2 minutes.

Add the potato and broccoli to the pan, stir well and add the stock cubes and 1 litre (35 fl oz/4 cups) water. Slowly bring to the boil, reduce the heat, cover and simmer over low heat for 20 minutes, or until the vegetables are tender. Allow to cool slightly.

Blend the soup in batches in a food processor or blender until smooth. Return to the pan and stir in the milk. Slowly reheat, without boiling. Stir the chopped coriander through and season well before serving.

Serves 6

Chilled tomato soup (Gazpacho)

2 slices day-old white crusty bread,
  crusts removed, broken into pieces
1 kg (2 lb 4 oz) vine-ripened tomatoes,
  peeled, seeded and chopped
1 red capsicum (pepper), seeded,
  roughly chopped
2 garlic cloves, chopped
1 small green chilli, chopped (optional)
1 teaspoon caster (superfine) sugar
2 tablespoons red wine vinegar
2 tablespoons extra virgin olive oil

Garnish
1/2 Lebanese (short) cucumber,
  seeded, finely diced
1/2 red capsicum (pepper), seeded,
  finely diced
1/2 green capsicum (pepper), seeded,
  finely diced
1/2 red onion, finely diced
1/2 ripe tomato, diced

Soak the bread in cold water for
5 minutes, then squeeze out any
excess liquid. put the bread in a food
processor with the tomato, capsicum,
garlic, chilli, sugar and vinegar, and
process until combined and smooth.

With the motor running, gradually add
the oil to make a smooth creamy
mixture. Season to taste. Refrigerate
for at least 2 hours. Add a little of the
extra vinegar, if desired.

To make the garnish, mix together
the ingredients. Spoon the chilled
gazpacho into soup bowls, top with
a little of the garnish and serve the
remaining garnish in separate bowls
on the side.

Serves 4

Broad bean soup

350 g (12 oz/2 cups) dried, skinned
and split broad (fava) beans or whole
dried broad (fava) beans
2 garlic cloves, peeled
1 teaspoon cumin
1 teaspoon paprika
extra virgin olive oil, cumin and paprika
to serve

Put the broad beans in a large bowl, cover with 3 times their volume of cold water and leave to soak in a cool place for 12 hours, drain and rinse before cooking. (If using whole beans soak for 48 hours in a cool place, changing water 3–4 times, drain and remove skins.)

Place beans in a large soup pot, preferably of stainless steel. Add 1.25 litres (44 fl oz/ 5 cups) cold water, garlic and spices. Bring to the boil and simmer on low heat, covered, for 45–60 minutes, until beans are mushy; check and add a little more water if beans look dry. Do not add salt or stir the beans during cooking.

Cool slightly and then purée soup in batches in a blender, or use a stick blender and purée in the pot. Reheat soup and season to taste. Ladle into bowls and drizzle a little olive oil on each serve. Finish with a light dusting of paprika. Have extra olive oil on the table, and cumin and paprika in little bowls, to be added to individual taste. Serve with bread.

Serves 6

Sides

Andalucian asparagus

500 g (1 lb 2 oz/32 spears) asparagus
1 thick slice of crusty, country-style
  bread
3 tablespoons extra virgin olive oil
2–3 garlic cloves
12 blanched almonds
1 teaspoon paprika
1 teaspoon ground cumin
1 tablespoon red wine vinegar or
  sherry vinegar

Trim woody ends from the asparagus.
Remove the crusts from the bread and
cut the bread into cubes.

Heat the olive oil in a frying pan.
Add the bread, garlic and almonds
and sauté over medium heat for
2–3 minutes, or until golden.

Using a slotted spoon, transfer the
mixture to a food processor. Add the
paprika, cumin, vinegar, 1 tablespoon
water and some sea salt and freshly
ground black pepper. Purée until the
mixture is finely chopped.

Return the frying pan to the heat and
add the asparagus, with a little extra
oil if necessary. Cook over medium
heat for 3–5 minutes, or until just
cooked, turning often. Transfer to a
serving plate.

Add the almond mixture to the pan
with 200 ml (7 fl oz) water. Simmer for
2–3 minutes, or until the liquid has
thickened slightly. Spoon over the
asparagus and serve.

Serves 4

Carrot timbales with creamy saffron and leek sauce

60 g (2¼ oz) butter
2 leeks, sliced
2 garlic cloves, crushed
1 kg (2 lb 4 oz) carrots, sliced
375 ml (13 fl oz/1½ cups) vegetable
  stock
1½ tablespoons finely chopped sage
3 tablespoons pouring (whipping)
  cream
4 eggs, lightly beaten

Creamy saffron and leek sauce
40 g (1½ oz) butter
1 small leek, finely sliced
1 large garlic clove, crushed
3 tablespoons dry white wine
pinch of saffron threads
90 g (3¼ oz/⅓ cup) crème fraîche

Preheat the oven to 170°C (325°F/ Gas 3). Lightly grease six 185 ml (6 fl oz/¾ cup) timbale moulds. Heat the butter in a saucepan and cook the leek for 3–4 minutes, or until soft. Add garlic and carrot and cook for a further 2–3 minutes. Pour in the stock and 500 ml (17 fl oz/2 cups) water, bring to the boil. Reduce the heat. Simmer, covered, for 5 minutes, or until the carrot is tender. Strain, reserving 185 ml (6 fl oz/¾ cup) of the liquid.

Blend the carrot mixture, 125 ml (4 fl oz/½ cup) of the reserved liquid and the sage in a food processor until smooth. Cool the mixture and stir in cream and egg. Season and pour into the moulds. Place moulds in roasting tin filled with hot water halfway up their sides. Bake for 30–40 minutes, or until just set.

To make sauce, melt the butter in a saucepan and cook the leek for 3–4 minutes without browning. Add the garlic and cook for 30 seconds. Add the wine, reserved liquid and saffron. Bring to the boil. Reduce the heat and simmer for 5 minutes, or until reduced. Stir in the crème fraîche.

Turn out the timbales onto serving plates and serve with the sauce.

Serves 6

Vegetable tempura with wasabi soy

Wasabi soy
4 tablespoons salt-reduced soy sauce
2 teaspoons wasabi paste

Tempura batter
150 g (5½ oz/1¼ cups) plain
   (all-purpose) flour
60 g (2¼ oz/½ cup) cornflour
   (cornstarch)
2 eggs

vegetable oil, for deep-frying
200 g (7 oz) orange sweet potato, cut
   into 1 cm (½ inch) thick slices
200 g (7 oz) carrots, cut into thick
   sticks
175 g (6 oz/11 spears) asparagus,
   trimmed, cut into 4–5 cm
   (1½–2 inch) pieces
100 g (3½ oz) green beans or snow
   peas (mangetout), trimmed
1 red capsicum (pepper), cut into
   large chunks

To make the wasabi soy, put the soy sauce and wasabi in a small bowl. Mix until well combined, then set aside.

To make the tempura batter, put the flour, cornflour and a pinch of salt in a large bowl. Mix well to combine. Whisk 250 ml (9 fl oz/1 cup) iced water and the eggs together. Add to the flour mixture and mix until just combined. Do not overmix, it doesn't matter if there are lumps in the batter.

Preheat the oven to 200°C (400°F/ Gas 6). Line a large baking tray with paper towel. Heat the oil in a large wide-based saucepan over medium– high heat until it reaches 180°C (350°F/Gas 4), or until a cube of bread dropped in the oil browns in 15 seconds. Dip the sweet potato into the batter, carefully shaking off any excess. Add to the oil and cook for 3–4 minutes, or until the batter is crisp and light golden. Use a slotted spoon to transfer to the paper towel. Once drained, transfer to the baking tray. Place in the oven to keep warm and crisp while repeating with the carrots, asparagus, beans and capsicum.

Serve the vegetable tempura immediately with wasabi soy.

Serves 4

Stuffed artichokes

40 g (1½ oz/¼ cup) raw almonds
4 young globe artichokes
150 g (5½ oz) fresh ricotta cheese
2 garlic cloves, crushed
80 g (2¾ oz/1 cup) fresh coarse
  breadcrumbs
1 teaspoon finely grated lemon zest
50 g (1¾ oz/½ cup) grated parmesan
  cheese
3 tablespoons chopped flat-leaf
  (Italian) parsley
1 tablespoon olive oil
2 tablespoons butter
2 tablespoons lemon juice

Preheat the oven to 180°C (350°F/ Gas 4). Spread the almonds on a baking tray. Bake for 5–10 minutes, or until lightly golden. Keep a close watch, as the almonds will burn easily. Cool, remove from the tray and chop.

Remove any tough outer leaves from the artichokes. Cut across the artichokes, about 3 cm (1¼ inches) from the top, and trim the stalks, leaving about 2 cm (¾ inch). Rub with lemon and put in a bowl of cold water with a little lemon juice to prevent the artichokes from turning brown.

Combine the almonds, ricotta, garlic, breadcrumbs, lemon zest, parmesan and parsley in a bowl and season. Gently separate the artichoke leaves and push the filling in between them.

Place the artichokes in a steamer and drizzle with the olive oil. Steam for 25–30 minutes, or until tender (test with a metal skewer). Remove and cook under a hot grill (broiler) for about 5 minutes to brown the filling.

Melt the butter in a saucepan, remove from the heat and stir in the lemon juice. Arrange the artichokes on a serving plate, drizzle with the butter sauce and season well.

Serves 4

Mushrooms baked with taleggio, herbs and garlic crumbs

1 tablespoon olive oil
8 (about 850 g/1 lb 14 oz) medium-
  large flat mushrooms, peeled
60 g (2¼ oz) butter, melted
½ leek, white part only, washed and
  thinly sliced
2 garlic cloves, finely chopped
2 tablespoons white wine
100 g (3½ oz/1¼ cups) fresh
  breadcrumbs
1 teaspoon thyme leaves
1 tablespoon flat-leaf (Italian) parsley,
  finely chopped, plus whole leaves,
  to serve
200 g (7 oz) taleggio cheese, cut into
  8 even slices

Preheat the oven to 180°C (350°F/ Gas 4). Brush a baking tray with the oil. Remove the stems from the mushrooms. Finely chop the stems and set the caps aside.

Heat 40 g (1½ oz) of the butter in a small frying pan over low heat and add the leek, garlic and mushroom stems. Cook, stirring often, for 5 minutes or until softened, then add the wine and cook for 3 minutes. Remove from the heat and place in a bowl, add the breadcrumbs, herbs and remaining butter. Season to taste with sea salt and freshly ground black pepper and mix well.

Place the mushroom caps on the prepared baking tray in a single layer, cap side up. Fill each cap with a slice of taleggio cheese, then divide the crumb mixture evenly among the mushrooms. Bake for 20 minutes, or until the mushrooms are tender and golden. Serve warm topped with parsley leaves.

Serves 4

Cauliflower fritters

600 g (1 lb 5 oz) cauliflower
55 g (2 oz/½ cup) besan (chickpea
  flour)
2 teaspoons ground cumin
1 teaspoon ground coriander
1 teaspoon ground turmeric
pinch cayenne pepper
1 egg, lightly beaten
1 egg yolk
oil, for deep-frying

Cut the cauliflower into bite-sized florets. Sift the flour and spices into a bowl, then stir in ½ teaspoon salt.

Lightly whisk the beaten egg, egg yolk and 60 ml (¼ cup) water in a jug. Make a well in the centre of the dry ingredients and pour in the egg mixture, whisking until smooth. Stand for 30 minutes.

Fill a deep saucepan one-third full of oil and heat to 180°C (350°F/Gas 4), or until a cube of bread dropped into the oil browns in 15 seconds. Dip the florets into the batter, allowing the excess to drain into the bowl. Deep-fry in batches for 3–4 minutes per batch, or until puffed and browned. Drain, sprinkle with salt and extra cayenne, if desired, and serve hot.

Serves 4–6

Zucchini flowers stuffed with Moroccan spiced chickpeas

150 g (5½ oz) butternut pumpkin
(squash), chopped
300 g (10½ oz) tinned chickpeas,
drained and rinsed
2 tablespoons currants
4 red Asian shallots, finely chopped
½ teaspoon ground cumin
½ teaspoon ground cinnamon
1½ tablespoons lemon juice
2 teaspoons chopped coriander
(cilantro) leaves
2 teaspoons chopped parsley
12 large zucchini (courgette) flowers
with stems attached

Garlic and lemon butter
100 g (3½ oz) ghee
4 garlic cloves, crushed
1 teaspoon ground coriander
pinch of cayenne pepper
1 tablespoon lemon juice

Place the pumpkin in a steamer and cover. Sit the steamer over a pan of boiling water and steam for 5–8 minutes, or until the pumpkin is soft. Transfer the pumpkin to a bowl, allow to cool then mash with a fork.

Meanwhile, mash the chickpeas in a separate bowl. Add the currants, shallots, cumin, cinnamon, lemon juice, herbs and season with salt and pepper. Fold the pumpkin through the mixture until well combined.

Remove the stamens from inside the zucchini flowers and trim the ends. Fill each flower until almost full, then gently twist the tips to secure the filling. Lay the stuffed flowers in the steamer so they all fit in a single layer.

Sit the steamer over a pan of boiling water and steam for 5–8 minutes, or until the zucchini are just tender.

Meanwhile, to make the butter, melt the ghee in a small pan over medium heat. Add the garlic and ½ teaspoon of salt and sauté for 2 minutes, or until the garlic starts to turn golden brown. Add the spices and cook 30 seconds. Stir in the lemon juice.

Put three zucchini flowers on each plate and drizzle with a little butter.

Serves 4

Vegetable pakoras with coriander chutney

650 g (1 lb 7 oz) selection of
  vegetables such as zucchini
  (courgette), red capsicum (pepper),
  orange sweet potato and onion
  (about 500 g/1 lb 2 oz peeled
  weight)

Chickpea batter
125 g (4½ oz/heaped 1 cup) besan
  (chickpea flour)
1 teaspoon salt
2 teaspoons curry powder
1 teaspoon ground turmeric
1 tablespoon sunflower oil
1 tablespoon lemon juice

Coriander chutney
4 large handfuls coriander (cilantro)
  leaves
1 large green chilli, deseeded and
  finely chopped
1 garlic clove, crushed
250 g (9 oz/1 cup) Greek-style yoghurt
1 tablespoon lemon juice

vegetable oil, for deep-frying

Peel and cut the vegetables into thin strips. Sift the besan into a bowl and stir in the salt, curry powder and turmeric. Make a well in the centre and gradually beat in the oil, lemon juice and 185 ml (6 fl oz/¾ cup) of water to make a smooth batter with the consistency of thick cream.

To make the chutney, put the coriander, chilli and garlic in a food processor with 2 tablespoons of cold water and process until smooth. Transfer to a bowl and stir in the yoghurt and lemon juice. Season to taste and set aside.

Heat 5 cm (2 inches) of vegetable oil in a wok or deep saucepan to 180°C (350°F/Gas 4), or until a cube of bread dropped in the oil browns in 15 seconds. Lightly whisk the batter and stir in the vegetables. Carefully slip bundles of batter-coated vegetables into the hot oil and fry in batches for 2–3 minutes, or until golden. Drain on paper towel and keep warm in the oven while cooking the remaining vegetables.

Serve the pakoras with the coriander chutney.

Serves 4

Spinach and leek fritters

40 g (1½ oz) butter
40 g (1½ oz/¼ cup) pine nuts
1 leek, white part only, thinly sliced
100 g (3½ oz) baby English spinach,
    chopped
3 eggs
1 egg yolk
1 tablespoon pouring (whipping)
    cream
70 g (2½ oz/¾ cup) grated parmesan
    cheese
1 tablespoon chopped parsley
1 tablespoon olive oil

Melt half the butter in a heavy-based frying pan over low–medium heat and cook the pine nuts and leek for 3 minutes, or until the pine nuts are golden. Add the spinach and cook for 1 minute. Remove the mixture from the pan and allow to cool slightly. Wipe out the pan with paper towels.

Whisk the eggs, yolk and cream together in a large bowl. Add the cheese and parsley and season with salt and freshly ground black pepper. Stir in the spinach mixture.

Melt half of the remaining butter and half of the oil in the frying pan. Place four 5–7 cm (2–2¾ inch) egg rings in the pan, and pour 60 ml (2 fl oz/ ¼ cup) of the spinach mixture into each. Cook over low heat for 2–3 minutes, or until the base is set. Gently flip and cook the other side for 2–3 minutes, or until firm. Transfer to a plate and slide out of the egg rings. Repeat with the remaining butter, oil and spinach mixture. Serve immediately.

Makes 8

Roasted root vegetables with caraway and garlic oil

2 bulbs beetroot (beets), cut into thick wedges
2 parsnips, cut in half lengthways
1 swede (rutabaga), cut into thick wedges
4 carrots, cut in half lengthways
1½ tablespoons caraway seeds
10 garlic cloves, unpeeled
3 tablespoons olive oil
2 slices day-old caraway bread, crusts removed (see Tip)
2 tablespoons roughly snipped garlic chives

Parboil the beetroot for 20 minutes, or until tender, then drain. Preheat the oven to 200°C (400°F/Gas 6).

In a large roasting pan, toss all the vegetables with the caraway seeds, garlic and 2 tablespoons oil. Season with salt and freshly ground black pepper. Roast for 30 minutes, then turn the vegetables. Reduce the heat to 180°C (350°F/Gas 4) and roast for a further 30–40 minutes, or until golden.

Meanwhile, brush the bread on both sides lightly with the remaining oil. Place on a baking tray and bake for 30 minutes, turning after 15 minutes, until crisp and golden. Cool, then break into chunky breadcrumbs.

Remove from the oven and serve on a platter sprinkled with the caraway breadcrumbs and garlic chives.

Serves 4

Tip: If you can't get caraway bread, use plain bread, and increase the caraway seeds to 2 tablespoons.

Grilled mixed mushrooms

2 field mushrooms
150 g (5½ oz/1½ punnets) fresh
  shiitake mushrooms
100 g (3½ oz/1 punnet) enoki
  mushrooms
150 g (5½ oz/1 punnet) oyster
  mushrooms
150 g (5½ oz/1 punnet) shimeji
  mushrooms
50 g (1¾ oz) butter, melted
2 tablespoons Japanese soy sauce
1 tablespoon mirin
1 tablespoon chopped flat-leaf (Italian)
  parsley

Heat the grill (broiler) to medium.
While the grill is heating, prepare the
mushrooms. Discard the stems from
the field mushrooms and cut the caps
into quarters. Discard the stems from
the shiitake mushrooms and cut the
shiitake in half. Trim the hard ends off
the enoki and pull apart the mushroom
tops. Gently tear apart the oyster
mushrooms. Remove the rough ends
from the shimeji stems and gently pull
apart the caps. Put all the mushrooms
in a large bowl.

Combine the butter, soy sauce and
mirin in a small bowl, pour over the
mushrooms and toss to combine.
Place the mushrooms in a shallow
ovenproof dish, put the dish under the
grill (broiler) and cook the mushrooms
for 5 minutes. Remove from the heat
and gently toss the mushrooms with a
pair of tongs, then grill (broil) for
another 5 minutes. Serve hot,
scattered with the parsley.

Serves 4

Parcels of snake beans with spiced peanuts

Spiced peanuts

80 g (2¾ oz/½ cup) toasted peanuts
1 garlic clove, finely chopped
1 tablespoon grated fresh ginger
½ teaspoon ground fennel
1 large red chilli, seeded and finely chopped
1 tablespoon grated palm sugar (jaggery) or soft brown sugar
1 tablespoon peanut oil
1 tablespoon lime juice
3 tablespoons fried shallots
2 tablespoons finely chopped coriander (cilantro) leaves

320 g (11¼ oz) snake (yard-long) beans, cut into 8 cm (3¼ inch) lengths
2 teaspoons sesame oil
12 garlic chives

Put the peanuts, garlic, ginger, ground fennel, chilli, palm sugar and ½ teaspoon of salt in a food processor. Blend until it reaches a coarse texture. Heat oil in a frying pan over medium–high heat. Add the peanut mixture and cook, stirring well, for 2–3 minutes, or until lightly brown and fragrant. Add the lime juice and fried shallots and cook for a further minute. Remove from the heat and set aside to cool. When the mixture has cooled a little, toss in the chopped coriander.

Meanwhile, put the snake beans in a steamer and cover with a lid. Sit the steamer over a wok or saucepan of boiling water and steam for 5 minutes, or until the beans are tender, then remove and set aside to cool a little. When the beans are cool enough to handle, toss with the sesame oil.

Bundle the beans into 12 even-sized parcels and tie together with a garlic chive. Place the beans on a serving platter and spoon the spiced peanuts over the top. Serve immediately.

Serves 6

Spiced potatoes

1.5 kg (3 lb 5 oz) roasting potatoes,
  peeled, cut into 4 cm (1½ inch)
  pieces
2 tablespoons ghee
2 teaspoons ground fenugreek
1 garlic clove, crushed
1 teaspoon finely grated fresh ginger
1 tablespoon black mustard seeds
pinch saffron threads
80 g (2¾ oz) baby English spinach
  leaves

Preheat oven to 180°C (350°F/Gas 4).
Boil, steam or microwave the potatoes
until just tender, then drain well.

Melt the ghee in a small frying pan
over medium heat. Cook the fenugreek,
garlic, ginger, mustard seeds and
saffron. Season with salt and stir, for
about 1 minute, or until fragrant.

Place the potatoes in a large roasting
tin, add the spice mixture and toss to
coat the potatoes. Bake for about
1 hour, or until the potatoes are lightly
browned. Remove from the oven, toss
the spinach through the potatoes and
serve immediately.

Serves 6

Baked sweet potato with saffron and pine nut butter

1 kg (2 lb 4 oz) white sweet potatoes
2 tablespoons vegetable oil
1 tablespoon milk
pinch saffron threads
100 g (3½ oz) unsalted butter,
  softened
40 g (1½ oz/¼ cup) pine nuts, toasted
2 tablespoons finely chopped parsley
2 garlic cloves, crushed

Preheat the oven to 180°C (350°F/ Gas 4). Peel the sweet potatoes and chop into large chunks. Toss to coat with oil. Place them on a baking tray, cover with foil and roast for 20 minutes.

Warm the milk, add the saffron and leave to infuse for 5 minutes. Put the butter, milk mixture, pine nuts, parsley and garlic in a food processor and pulse to combine. Take care not to overprocess, the nuts should still have some texture. Place a sheet of plastic wrap on the workbench, put the butter in the centre and roll up to form a neat log, about 4 cm (1½ inches) in diameter. Refrigerate the butter for half an hour.

Remove the foil from the potatoes and roast, uncovered, for another 30 minutes, or until they are cooked through (test this by piercing with a skewer). Bring the butter to room temperature, unwrap, cut into 1 cm (½ inch) slices and return to the refrigerator to keep cool.

Arrange the butter slices over the sweet potato, season with salt and freshly ground black pepper and serve.

Serves 4–6

Grilled eggplant with miso and parmesan

6 slender eggplants (aubergines)
2 teaspoons olive oil
1½ tablespoons white miso paste
1 tablespoon mirin
1 egg yolk
2 tablespoons finely grated parmesan
  cheese
2 tablespoons snipped chives

Heat the grill (broiler) to high. Slice the eggplants in half lengthways and prick the skins several times with a fork. Brush the eggplant with the oil, place skin-side-up on the grill tray and grill (broil) for 10 minutes, turning once.

Remove eggplant from the grill and arrange in a shallow ovenproof serving dish. Turn the grill down to medium.

Put the miso paste, mirin and egg yolk in a small bowl and whisk well to combine. Pour the mixture evenly over the surface of the eggplant and put the dish under the grill. Cook for 2 minutes, then sprinkle with the parmesan and grill for 1 minute more, or until the cheese starts to turn golden. Sprinkle with chives and serve.

Serves 4

Zucchini wrapped in prosciutto

2 small green zucchini (courgettes)
2 small yellow zucchini (courgettes)
8 thin slices prosciutto

Sage butter
40 g (1½ oz) butter, softened
1 tablespoon finely chopped sage
1 tablespoon finely chopped semi-
    dried (sun-blushed) tomatoes

Preheat a barbecue hotplate to low. Meanwhile, bring a large saucepan of water to the boil. Add the whole zucchini, then reduce the heat and simmer for 5 minutes, or until almost tender. Drain well, allow to cool, then pat dry with paper towels.

To make the sage butter, put the butter, sage and tomato in a small bowl and mix well. Season to taste with salt and freshly ground black pepper and set aside until needed.

Wrap 2 slices of prosciutto around each zucchini — it should stick together quite easily. Put the zucchini on the hotplate and cook for about 15 minutes, or until cooked through, turning halfway through cooking and keeping a close watch to ensure they don't burn. Serve hot, with a dollop of sage butter.

Makes 4

Fennel with pecorino cheese

4 fennel bulbs
1 garlic clove, crushed
1/2 lemon, sliced
2 tablespoons olive oil
3 tablespoons butter, melted
2 tablespoons grated pecorino cheese
   (see Note)

Cut the top shoots and base off the fennel and remove the tough outer layers. Cut into segments and place in a saucepan with the garlic, lemon, oil and 1 teaspoon of salt. Cover with water and bring to the boil. Reduce the heat and simmer for 20 minutes, or until just tender.

Drain well and place in a flameproof dish. Drizzle with the butter. Sprinkle with the cheese and season to taste.

Place under a preheated grill (broiler) until the cheese has browned. Best served piping hot.

Serves 4

Note: If pecorino (a hard sheep's milk cheese) is not available, then use parmesan cheese instead.

Potato gratin

30 g (1 oz) butter
1 onion, halved and thinly sliced
650 g (1 lb 7 oz) floury potatoes,
thinly sliced
90 g (3¼ oz/⅔ cup) grated
cheddar cheese
300 ml (10½ fl oz) pouring
(whipping) cream
100 ml (3½ fl oz) milk

Heat the butter in a frying pan and
cook the onion over low heat for
5 minutes, or until it is soft and
translucent.

Preheat the oven to 160°C (315°F/
Gas 3). Grease the base and sides
of a deep 1 litre (35 fl oz/4 cup)
ovenproof dish. Layer the potato
slices with the onion and cheese
(reserving 2 tablespoons of cheese
for the top). Whisk together the cream
and milk, and season with salt and
freshly ground black pepper. Slowly
pour over the potato, then sprinkle
with the remaining cheese.

Bake for 50–60 minutes, or until
golden brown and the potato is very
soft. Leave to rest for 10 minutes
before serving.

Serves 4

Variation: For something different, try
combining potato and orange sweet
potato, layering alternately. For extra
flavour, add chopped fresh herbs to
the cream and milk mixture.

Cabbage with leek and mustard seeds

1 tablespoon oil
2 tablespoons unsalted butter
2 teaspoons black mustard seeds
2 leeks, washed and thinly sliced
500 g (1 lb 2 oz) thinly shredded
  cabbage
1 tablespoon lemon juice
5 tablespoons crème fraîche
2 tablespoons chopped parsley

Heat the oil and butter together, add the mustard seeds, and cook until they start to pop. Add the leeks and cook gently for 5-8 minutes, or until softened. Stir in the cabbage and cook over low heat for 4 minutes, or until it wilts and softens.

Season the cabbage well with salt and freshly ground black pepper. Add the lemon juice and crème fraîche, and cook for 1 minute longer. Stir in chopped parsley and serve immediately.

Serves 4-6

Golden nugget pumpkins with goat's cheese and macadamia nuts

2 x 350 g (12 oz) golden nugget
  pumpkins (minikin squash)
1 tablespoon oil
40 g (1½ oz) baby rocket (arugula)
  leaves
35 g (1¼ oz/¼ cup) chopped roasted
  macadamia nuts
80 g (2¾ oz/⅔ cup) goat's cheese,
  crumbled

Honey mustard dressing
3 tablespoons olive oil
1 tablespoon sherry vinegar
2 teaspoons wholegrain mustard
1 teaspoon honey

Preheat a covered barbecue to medium indirect heat.

Wash the pumpkins thoroughly, then cut them in half horizontally and remove all the seeds. Rub the oil all over the flesh and place the pumpkins cut-side-up in a disposable foil tray. Season lightly with salt and freshly ground black pepper. Put the tray on the barbecue grill (hotplate), then lower the lid and cook for 30 minutes, or until browned and soft — the cooking time will depend on the thickness of your pumpkins.

Meanwhile, put all the honey mustard dressing ingredients in a small screw-top jar. Shake well to combine and season to taste with salt and freshly ground black pepper.

Put the rocket, macadamia nuts and goat's cheese in a large bowl and gently mix together. Add the dressing and toss lightly to combine. Fill the cooked pumpkin halves with the salad mixture and serve immediately.

Tip: The skin of the pumpkins can be eaten in this recipe — just be sure to wash the pumpkins well before cooking.

Serves 4

Potato and sage chips

2 large all-purpose potatoes
2 tablespoons olive oil
25 sage leaves
sea salt, for sprinkling

Preheat the oven to 200°C (400°F/ Gas 6). Using a large sharp knife or a mandoline, cut the potatoes lengthways to give 50 paper-thin slices. Toss the slices in the olive oil.

Line two baking trays with baking paper. Sandwich a sage leaf between two slices of potato and sprinkle with sea salt. Repeat with the remaining potatoes and sage leaves.

Arrange on the baking trays in a single layer and bake for 25–30 minutes, or until the chips are browned and crisp, turning once — watch carefully during cooking so they don't burn (some chips may cook slightly more quickly than others). Serve hot.

Serves 4

Finnish creamy baked swede

1.6 kg (3 lb 8 oz/about 4) swedes
(rutabaga), peeled and cut into 4 cm
(1½ inch) pieces
125 ml (4 fl oz/½ cup) pouring
(whipping) cream
2 eggs, lightly beaten
1 egg yolk
3 tablespoons plain (all-purpose) flour
½ teaspoon freshly grated nutmeg
a small pinch of ground cloves
100 g (3½ oz/1¼ cups) fresh
breadcrumbs
50 g (1¾ oz) unsalted butter, chopped
4 sage leaves, finely chopped

Preheat the oven to 180°C (350°F/
Gas 4). Grease a shallow 18 x 30 cm
(7 x 12 inch) baking dish.

Cook the swedes in boiling salted
water for 40 minutes, or steam them
for 25 minutes, until tender. Drain well
and return to the saucepan, then mash
well using a potato masher — the
mixture should still have some texture.

Place the saucepan back over
medium heat and cook the swede,
stirring often, for 5–7 minutes, or until
the excess liquid has evaporated.
Remove from the heat and allow to
cool slightly.

Stir in the cream, eggs, egg yolk, flour
and spices, then season with sea salt
and freshly ground black pepper. Pour
the mixture into the baking dish,
smoothing the top even.

Put breadcrumbs and butter in a food
processor and blend until fine clumps
form, then add the sage and sprinkle
the mixture over the swede. Bake for
30–35 minutes, or until golden and set
in the middle. Serve hot or warm as a
side dish to accompany roasted or
grilled (broiled) meats.

Serves 6–8

Creamy celeriac parcels

125 ml (4 fl oz/½ cup) dry white wine
125 ml (4 fl oz/½ cup) pouring
(whipping) cream
1 teaspoon ground cumin
1 tablespoon wholegrain mustard
1 celeriac, weighing about 600 g
(1 lb 5 oz), peeled and finely sliced,
then cut into thin strips

Preheat the oven to 180°C (350°F/
Gas 4). Combine the wine, cream,
cumin and mustard in a bowl and
season well with salt and freshly
ground black pepper. Add the celeriac
and toss well to coat. Leave for a
couple of minutes.

Meanwhile, cut four 50 cm (20 inch)
lengths of baking paper. Divide the
mixture into four and place it in the
middle of each piece (it's easiest to
do this using your hands). Spoon any
remaining cream mixture over the top.
Seal parcels by bringing the two long
sides up over the celeriac and folding
the edges over a few times. Then twist
the ends tightly together and tuck the
ends under. It's important that the
packages are sealed tightly, otherwise
the celeriac won't steam properly.

Put parcels on one or two baking trays
and bake for 45 minutes, or until the
celeriac is tender. Leave to cool slightly
for a couple of minutes before opening.
Delicious served with roast meats.

Serves 4

Vegetable tian

1 kg (2 lb 4 oz) red capsicums
(peppers)
125 ml (4 fl oz/½ cup) olive oil
2 tablespoons pine nuts
800 g (1 lb 10 oz) silverbeet (Swiss
chard), stems removed and the
leaves coarsely shredded
freshly ground nutmeg, to taste
1 onion, chopped
2 garlic cloves
2 teaspoons chopped thyme
750 g (1 lb 10 oz) tomatoes, peeled,
seeded and diced
1 large eggplant (aubergine), cut into
1 cm (½ inch) rounds
5 small zucchini (courgettes), about
500 g (1 lb 2 oz) in total, thinly sliced
on the diagonal
3 ripe tomatoes, cut into 1 cm
(½ inch) slices
1 tablespoon fresh breadcrumbs
4 tablespoons grated parmesan
cheese
30 g (1 oz) unsalted butter, chopped

Preheat grill (broiler) to high. Quarter
the capsicums. Remove the seeds and
membranes. Grill (broil) the capsicums,
skin side up, until skin blackens. Move
to a bowl, cover and let cool. Slip the
skin off the capsicums, then cut the
flesh into strips. Place in a greased
25 x 20 x 5 cm (10 x 8 x 2 inch) baking
dish and season.

Preheat the oven to 200°C (400°F/
Gas 6). Heat 2 tablespoons of the
oil in a pan. Add the nuts and fry
for 1–2 minutes. Remove and set
aside. Add the silverbeet and cook for
5 minutes. Add the nuts and season.
Spread the mixture over the capsicum.

Heat another tablespoon of the oil.
Add the onion and cook over medium
heat for 7–8 minutes. Add the garlic
and thyme, cook for 1 minute. Add the
tomato. Bring to the boil, reduce the
heat and simmer for 10 minutes.
Spread the sauce over the silverbeet.

Heat the remaining oil. Add the
eggplant. Cook on each side for
4–5 minutes. Drain on paper towels
and place in a single layer over the
sauce. Season. Layer the zucchini and
tomato over the eggplant. Sprinkle the
breadcrumbs and parmesan on top,
then dot with the butter. Bake for
25–30 minutes. Serve warm.

Serves: 6–8

Braised celery

30 g (1 oz) unsalted butter
1 bunch of celery, trimmed and cut
  into 5 cm (2 inch) lengths
500 ml (17 fl oz/2 cups) chicken or
  vegetable stock
2 teaspoons finely grated lemon zest
3 tablespoons lemon juice
3 tablespoons pouring (whipping)
  cream
2 egg yolks
1 tablespoon cornflour (cornstarch)
a pinch of ground mace or nutmeg
1–2 tablespoons chopped parsley

Preheat the oven to 180°C (350°F/ Gas 4). Grease a large shallow baking dish. Melt the butter in a large frying pan. Add the celery, toss to coat evenly in the butter, then cover and cook over medium heat for 2 minutes.

Pour in the stock. Add the lemon zest and lemon juice, then cover and simmer for 10 minutes, or until the celery is tender, but still holds its shape. Remove the celery using a slotted spoon and place in the baking dish. Reserve 3 tablespoons of the cooking liquid.

In a bowl, mix together the cream, egg yolks and cornflour. Whisk in the reserved cooking liquid. Pour the mixture back into the frying pan and cook, stirring constantly, until the mixture boils and thickens. Add the mace and season to taste with sea salt and freshly ground black pepper.

Pour the sauce over the celery and bake for 15 minutes, or until the celery is very soft and the sauce is bubbling. Scatter the parsley over the top.

Serve warm with poached chicken breast, chargrilled lamb or slices of corned beef.

Serves 4

Zucchini patties

Cucumber and yoghurt salad
1 Lebanese (short) cucumber
sea salt, for sprinkling
250 g (9 oz/1 cup) Greek-style yoghurt
1 small garlic clove, crushed
1 tablespoon chopped dill
2 teaspoons white wine vinegar
ground white pepper, to taste

300 g (10 oz) zucchini (courgettes),
   grated
1 small onion, finely chopped
3 tablespoons self-raising flour
4 tablespoons grated kefalotyri
   or parmesan cheese
1 tablespoon chopped mint
2 teaspoons chopped flat-leaf (Italian)
   parsley
a pinch of ground nutmeg
3 tablespoons dry breadcrumbs
1 egg, lightly beaten
olive oil, for pan-frying
rocket (arugula) leaves, to serve
lemon wedges, to serve (optional)

To make the cucumber and yoghurt salad, chop the cucumber into small pieces, place in a colander, sprinkle with sea salt and set aside in the sink to drain for 15–20 minutes.

In a bowl, mix the yoghurt, garlic, dill and vinegar. Add the cucumber and season to taste with salt and ground white pepper. Cover and refrigerate until required. Meanwhile, preheat the oven to 120ºC (235ºF/Gas ½).

Put the zucchini and onion in a clean tea towel (dish towel), gather the corners together and twist tightly to remove all the juices. Tip the zucchini and onion into a large bowl, then add the flour, cheese, herbs, nutmeg, breadcrumbs and egg. Season well with sea salt and pepper, then mix with your hands to a stiff batter.

Heat 1 cm (½ inch) oil in a heavy-based pan over medium heat. When the oil is hot, drop 2 tablespoons of the batter into the pan and press flat to make a patty. Fry several at a time for 2–3 minutes, or until well browned. Drain on paper towels and place in the oven while cooking the other patties.

Serve hot with rocket leaves and the cucumber and yoghurt salad, and perhaps some lemon wedges.

Serves 4

Brussels sprouts with pancetta

100 g (3½ oz) pancetta, thinly sliced
4 shallots
20 g (¾ oz) butter
1 tablespoon olive oil
1 garlic clove, crushed
500 g (1 lb 2 oz) brussels sprouts, trimmed and thickly sliced

Preheat the oven grill (broiler) to high. Spread the pancetta on a baking tray lined with foil and place 8–10 cm (3¼–4 inches) under the heat. Grill (broil) for 1 minute, or until crisp, then set aside to cool.

Put the shallots in a saucepan of boiling water for 5 minutes to make them easier to peel. Remove the shallots using a slotted spoon, allow to cool slightly, then peel and cut into thick rings.

Heat the butter and olive oil in a large frying pan. Add the shallot and garlic and sauté over medium heat for 3–4 minutes, or until just starting to brown. Add the brussels sprouts and season with freshly ground black pepper. Sauté for 4–5 minutes, or until the brussels sprouts are light golden and crisp. Turn off the heat, cover and set aside for 5 minutes.

Break the pancetta into large pieces, gently toss through the vegetables and serve.

Serves 4

Fennel crumble

100 ml (3½ fl oz) lemon juice
2 fennel bulbs, or 5 baby fennel bulbs
1 tablespoon honey
1 tablespoon plain (all-purpose) flour
310 ml (10¾ fl oz/1¼ cups) pouring
  (whipping) cream

Crumble topping
75 g (2½ oz/¾ cup) rolled (porridge)
  oats
60 g (2¼ oz/½ cup) plain (all-purpose)
  flour
110 g (3¾ oz/1 cup) fresh black rye
  breadcrumbs (see Note)
60 g (2¼ oz) unsalted butter
1 garlic clove, crushed

Preheat the oven to 180°C (350°F/
Gas 4). Grease a large heatproof
serving dish.

Bring a large saucepan of water to
the boil and add 3 tablespoons of the
lemon juice. Trim the fennel and cut
into thin slices. Wash and drain well,
then add to the boiling water and cook
over medium heat for 3 minutes. Drain
well and allow to cool slightly.

Put the fennel in a large bowl. Add the
honey and remaining lemon juice and
season with freshly ground black
pepper. Sprinkle with the flour and
toss to combine. Spoon into the
prepared dish and pour the cream
over the top.

To make the crumble topping, put
the oats, flour and breadcrumbs in
a bowl. Melt the butter in a small
saucepan, add the garlic and cook
for 30 seconds. Pour over the dry
ingredients and mix well.

Sprinkle the crumble topping over
the fennel. Bake for 20–30 minutes,
or until the fennel is tender and the
topping is nicely browned. Serve hot.

Serves 6

Note: White or wholemeal (whole-
wheat) breadcrumbs can be used in
place of rye bread, if preferred.

Beetroot with skordalia

1 kg (2 lb 4 oz) beetroot (beets), with
  leaves attached
3 tablespoons extra virgin olive oil
1 tablespoon red wine vinegar

Skordalia
250 g (9 oz) roasting potatoes, such
  as russet (idaho) or king edward,
  peeled and cut into 2 cm (3/4 inch)
  cubes
2–3 garlic cloves, crushed
1/2 teaspoon sea salt
ground white pepper, to taste
90 ml (3 fl oz) olive oil
1 tablespoon white vinegar

Cut the stems from the beetroot,
leaving 2–3 cm (3/4–1 1/4 inches)
attached. Wash the leaves, discarding
any tough outer ones. Cut the stems
and leaves into 7 cm (2 3/4 inch) lengths
and wash well. Scrub the bulbs clean.

Bring a large saucepan of salted water
to the boil. Add the bulbs and gently
boil for 30–45 minutes, or until tender
when pierced with a skewer. Remove
with a slotted spoon and cool slightly.

Meanwhile, make the skordalia. Bring
a saucepan of water to the boil, add
the potato and cook for 10 minutes,
or until very soft. Drain well, then
mash until quite smooth. Stir in the
garlic, sea salt and a pinch of white
pepper, then gradually add the olive
oil, stirring well with a wooden spoon.
Stir in the vinegar and season to taste.

Bring the beetroot water back to
the boil. Add the leaves and boil for
8 minutes, or until tender. Drain well,
allow to cool slightly, then squeeze out
any excess water from the leaves.

Peel the beetroot, then cut into
quarters. Arrange on a serving plate
with the leaves. Mix together the extra
virgin olive oil and vinegar, season to
taste and drizzle over the leaves and
bulbs. Serve warm with the skordalia.

Serves 6

Leeks a la grecque

3 tablespoons extra virgin olive oil
1½ tablespoons white wine
1 tablespoon tomato paste
   (concentrated purée)
¼ teaspoon sugar
1 bay leaf
1 thyme sprig
1 garlic clove, crushed
4 coriander seeds, crushed
4 peppercorns
8 small leeks, white part only, rinsed
   well
1 teaspoon lemon juice
sea salt, to taste
1 tablespoon chopped parsley
lemon halves or wedges, to serve

Put the olive oil, wine, tomato paste, sugar, bay leaf, thyme, garlic, coriander seeds, peppercorns and 250 ml (9 fl oz/1 cup) water in a large heavy-based frying pan with a lid. Bring to the boil, cover and simmer for 5 minutes.

Add the leeks in a single layer and bring to simmering point. Reduce the heat, then cover and simmer gently for 20–30 minutes, or until the leeks are tender when pierced with a skewer. Drain the leeks well, reserving the liquid, then transfer to a serving dish.

Add the lemon juice to the reserved cooking liquid and boil rapidly for 1 minute, or until the liquid has reduced and is slightly syrupy. Season to taste with sea salt, then strain the sauce over the leeks.

Allow to cool, then serve the leeks at room temperature, sprinkled with chopped parsley and with some lemon for squeezing over.

Serves 4

Chargrilled radicchio

2 radicchio
3 tablespoons olive oil
sea salt, to taste
1 teaspoon balsamic vinegar

Trim the radicchio, discarding outer leaves. Slice the heads into quarters lengthways and rinse well. Drain well, then pat dry with paper towels.

Heat a chargrill pan or barbecue chargrill plate to high. Lightly drizzle the radicchio with some of the oil and season with salt and freshly ground black pepper. Cook for 2–3 minutes, or until the outer leaves soften and darken, then turn to cook the other side. Transfer to a dish and sprinkle with the remaining oil and vinegar.

Serve hot with grilled (broiled) meats, or at room temperature as part of an antipasti platter.

Serves 4

Moroccan spiced carrot salad

4 large carrots
2 cardamom pods
1 teaspoon black mustard seeds
1/2 teaspoon ground cumin
1/2 teaspoon ground ginger
1 teaspoon paprika
1/2 teaspoon ground coriander
80 ml (2½ fl oz/⅓ cup) olive oil
1 tablespoon lemon juice
2 tablespoons orange juice
35 g (1¼ oz/¼ cup) currants
25 g (1 oz/½ cup) finely chopped
  coriander (cilantro)
2 tablespoons finely chopped
  pistachio nuts
1 teaspoon orange flower water
250 g (9 oz/1 cup) thick plain yoghurt

Peel and coarsely grate the carrots, and place in a large bowl.

Crush the cardamom pods to extract the seeds. Discard the pods. Heat a frying pan over low heat, and cook the mustard seeds for a few seconds, or until they start to pop. Add the cumin, ginger, paprika, cardamom and ground coriander, and heat for 5 seconds, or until fragrant. Remove from the heat and stir in the oil, juices and currants until combined.

Pour the dressing over the carrot and leave for 30 minutes. Add the fresh coriander and toss to combine. Pile the salad onto a serving dish and garnish with the chopped pistachios. Mix the orange flower water and yoghurt, and serve separately.

Serves 4–6

Baked onions stuffed with goat's cheese and sun-dried tomatoes

6 large onions
60 ml (2 fl oz/¼ cup) extra virgin olive oil
1 garlic clove, crushed
100 g (3½ oz) sun-dried tomatoes, finely chopped
25 g (1 oz/⅓ cup) fresh white breadcrumbs
1 tablespoon chopped parsley
2 teaspoons chopped thyme
100 g (3½ oz) mild soft goat's cheese, crumbled
80 g (3 oz/¾ cup) parmesan cheese, grated
1 egg
250 ml (9 fl oz/1 cup) vegetable or chicken stock
1 tablespoon butter

Preheat the oven to 180°C (350°F/ Gas 4). Peel the onions, cut a slice off the top and reserve. Using a teaspoon scrape out a cavity almost to the base of the onion, leaving a hole to stuff.

Blanch the onions in a large saucepan of boiling water for 5 minutes, then drain. Heat 2 tablespoons of oil in a small frying pan and cook the garlic for 3 minutes, or until soft. Add the tomato, breadcrumbs and herbs and cook for 1 minute. Remove from the heat and add the goat's cheese and parmesan. Season and stir in the egg.

Stuff the mixture into each onion cavity. Arrange the onions in a large ovenproof ceramic dish. Pour the stock around the onions and drizzle with the remaining oil. Cover with foil and bake for 45 minutes, basting from time to time. Remove the foil for the last 10 minutes of cooking.

Remove the onions to a serving plate and, over medium heat, simmer the remaining stock for 5–8 minutes, or until reduced by half and syrupy. Reduce the heat and whisk in the butter. The sauce should be smooth and glossy. Season to taste and spoon over the onions.

Serves 6

Couscous with grilled fennel

4 baby fennel bulbs, with fronds
olive oil, for brushing
2 red onions, each cut into 8 wedges
250 ml (9 fl oz/1 cup) chicken or
  vegetable stock
140 g (5 oz/³/₄ cup) couscous

Preserved lemon dressing
1 preserved lemon quarter
4 tablespoons virgin olive oil
½ teaspoon dijon mustard
1½ tablespoons lemon juice

Bring a saucepan of water to the boil. Meanwhile, trim the fronds from the fennel bulbs. Chop up a tablespoon of fronds and reserve. Remove the stalks from the fennel and cut a 5 mm (¼ inch) thick slice off the base of each bulb. Cut the bulbs into quarters, then add them to the pan of boiling water. Cook, covered, for about 3 minutes, or until tender. Drain well.

Heat the grill (broiler) to medium. Lightly brush the tray with oil and spread the fennel and onion wedges over the top. Brush with a little olive oil and grill (broil) for 10 minutes, or until tender, turning during cooking.

Meanwhile, make the preserved lemon dressing. Scoop out and discard the flesh from the lemon. Wash the rind well, then pat dry and finely chop. In a small bowl, whisk the oil, mustard and lemon juice until combined. Add the preserved lemon and season to taste.

To prepare the couscous, bring the stock to the boil in a saucepan. Stir in the couscous and reserved fronds and take the pan off the heat. Cover and leave for 4–5 minutes, then fluff up the couscous with a fork. Transfer the couscous to a serving dish and arrange the grilled wedges over the top. Drizzle with dressing and serve.

Serves 4

Cauliflower and peas with a polonaise topping

1 small cauliflower, cut into small
  florets
150 g (5½ oz/1 cup) fresh or frozen
  peas (see Tip)

Polonaise topping
3 hard-boiled eggs
40 g (1½ oz/½ cup) fresh white
  breadcrumbs
1½ tablespoons baby capers, rinsed
  and drained
3 tablespoons finely chopped flat-leaf
  (Italian) parsley
1 garlic clove, finely chopped
75 g (2½ oz) unsalted butter, melted

Heat the grill (broiler) to high. Add the cauliflower and peas to a large saucepan of lightly salted boiling water and simmer for about 5 minutes, or until tender. Drain the vegetables and arrange in a lightly oiled 26 x 18 cm (10½ x 7 inch) gratin dish.

While the vegetables are cooking, make the polonaise topping. Mash the eggs in a bowl using a fork, then add the breadcrumbs, capers, parsley, garlic and melted butter. Mix well and season to taste with salt and freshly ground black pepper. Sprinkle the topping all over the vegetables and grill (broil) for about 5–7 minutes, or until the breadcrumbs are golden and crunchy. Serve hot.

Serves 4

Tip: If you prefer to use fresh peas in this recipe, you will need to pod about 300 g (10½ oz) fresh peas to get the right amount.

Feta-filled zucchini

6 zucchini (courgettes)
250 g (9 oz) feta cheese, crumbled
2 tablespoons snipped chives
1 garlic clove, crushed
2$\frac{1}{2}$ tablespoons olive oil
6 lemon wedges

Put the whole zucchini in a saucepan of salted, boiling water and cook for about 6 minutes, or until just tender. Drain and leave to cool slightly.

Heat the grill (broiler) to high. Put the feta, chives and garlic in a small bowl with 1 tablespoon of the oil and freshly cracked black pepper to taste. Mix well.

When the zucchini are cool enough to handle, slice a strip about 5 mm ($\frac{1}{4}$ inch) deep from along the length of each zucchini and discard. Use a teaspoon to scoop out most of the seeds, and sit the zucchini cut-side-up on a lightly oiled baking tray.

Spoon equal amounts of the feta mixture into the cavity of each zucchini. Lightly brush each zucchini with a little of the oil and grill (broil) for about 10 minutes, or until lightly browned. Drizzle with the remaining oil, sprinkle with freshly cracked black pepper and serve with the lemon wedges.

Serves 6

Tip: This recipe can be prepared a day or two in advance. You can reheat the zucchini and serve them warm, but they are also delicious simply served cold on an antipasto platter.

Barbecued corn cakes

125 g (4½ oz/1 cup) plain
(all-purpose) flour
75 g (2½ oz/½ cup) fine polenta
1 teaspoon baking powder
1 egg
170 ml (5½ oz/⅔ cup) buttermilk
1 cooked corn cob, kernels cut off
1 tablespoon chopped pickled
jalapeño chilli
1 large red chilli, seeded and chopped
1 tablespoon chopped coriander
(cilantro) leaves
1 tablespoon chopped parsley
olive oil, for brushing

Tomato and avocado relish
4 roma (plum) tomatoes, quartered
1 tablespoon lime juice
1 avocado, cut into 2 cm (¾ inch)
cubes

Preheat a barbecue grill plate or flat plate to medium. Put the flour, polenta, baking powder and 1 teaspoon of salt in a large bowl, making a well in the centre. In a small bowl, whisk together the egg and buttermilk, then pour into the flour mixture and stir to thoroughly combine. Mix through the corn, chilli, coriander and parsley.

Brush the barbecue hotplate with 1 tablespoon of oil. Cook the tomato quarters for 2 minutes on each side, then remove and allow to cool. To make the tomato and avocado relish, roughly chop the cooled tomato and place in a bowl with the lime juice and ½ teaspoon salt. Add the avocado cubes, mix gently and set aside.

Brush the barbecue hotplate with a tablespoon of oil. Spoon 2 tablespoons of corn cake batter onto the hotplate to form a round cake, then repeat until the batter is used up — you should have enough to make 12 corn cakes. Cook for 2 minutes, or until bubbles appear on the surface. Turn and cook for a further 2–3 minutes, or until golden brown, brushing the hotplate with more oil if necessary. Serve the corn cakes hot, with the tomato and avocado relish on the side.

Makes 12

Pumpkin with saffron and coriander butter

Saffron and coriander butter
small pinch of saffron threads
50 g (1¾ oz) butter, softened
1 tablespoon finely chopped coriander
  (cilantro) leaves

½ jap (kent) pumpkin
olive oil, for brushing
3 tablespoons coriander (cilantro)
  leaves

To make the saffron and coriander butter, put the saffron in a small bowl, add 2 teaspoons of hot water and leave to soak for at least 20 minutes. Add the butter and coriander and mix until thoroughly combined. Put the butter mixture into the centre of a piece of plastic wrap, then roll up into a 7 cm (2¾ inch) log. Refrigerate for about 30 minutes, or until firm.

Preheat a barbecue grill plate or chargrill pan to high. Slice the unpeeled pumpkin into 2 cm (¾ inch) thick wedges and discard the seeds. Brush the wedges on both sides with oil and season with salt and freshly ground black pepper.

Cook the pumpkin for 10 minutes on each side, or until browned and tender. Place on a serving platter and top with the sliced saffron and coriander butter. Allow the butter to melt a little and serve the pumpkin hot, scattered with coriander leaves.

Serves 6

Skewered garlic and cumin mushrooms

16 button mushrooms
4 tablespoons olive oil
1 garlic clove, crushed
1/2 teaspoon ground cumin
2 tablespoons chopped parsley
1 lemon, cut into 4 wedges

Soak four bamboo skewers in cold water for 30 minutes. Preheat a barbecue grill plate, flat plate or chargrill pan to medium.

Trim the ends of the mushroom stalks, but don't cut them off completely. Put the oil, garlic, cumin and some salt and cracked black pepper in a bowl. Add the mushrooms and toss to coat.

Thread 4 mushrooms onto each skewer, piercing them through the stalk. Barbecue the mushrooms, turning occasionally and brushing with any remaining oil mixture, for about 5 minutes, or until soft and lightly browned. Place on a serving plate, sprinkle with parsley, add a squeeze of lemon and serve.

Serves 4

Baby fennel with lemon and anchovy butter

4 baby fennel bulbs
60 g (2¼ oz) butter
8 anchovy fillets, finely chopped
1 garlic clove, crushed
2 small red chillies, seeded and finely
  chopped
2 tablespoons lemon juice

Cut stems off the fennel bulbs, then cut the bulbs lengthways into quarters.

Put them in a steamer and cover with a lid. Sit the steamer over a saucepan or wok of simmering water and steam for 5 minutes, or until tender.

Melt the butter in a frying pan over medium heat, add the anchovy, garlic and chilli and cook, stirring, for 30 seconds. Stir in the lemon juice, add fennel and toss until combined.

Serves 4

Witlof with cheese and pecan topping

4 witlof (chicory/Belgian endive), large
   outer leaves removed, then halved
80 g (2¾ oz/1 cup) fresh breadcrumbs
3 tablespoons grated parmesan
   cheese
3 tablespoons chopped pecans
1 tablespoon chopped thyme
1 tablespoon snipped chives
3 slices of prosciutto, roughy chopped
60 g (2¼ oz) butter, melted

Put the witlof halves in a large steamer and cover with a lid. Sit the steamer over a saucepan or wok of boiling water and steam for 15 minutes, or until tender (test by inserting a skewer into the thickest part). Transfer to a baking tray, cut side up.

Preheat the oven to 200°C (400°F/ Gas 6). Combine the breadcrumbs, cheese, pecans, thyme, chives and prosciutto in a bowl, then stir in the butter. Spoon the mixture over the cut side of the witlof, pressing down lightly. Bake for 10 minutes, or until golden and crunchy.

Serves 4

Tip: The witlof can be cooked in advance up until the stage of topping them with the breadcrumb mixture. Refrigerate until needed, then top with the mixture and bake just before serving.

Brussels sprouts in mustard butter

500 g (1 lb 2 oz) brussels sprouts
30 g (1 oz) butter
3 teaspoons wholegrain mustard
2 teaspoons honey

Trim the ends and remove any loose leaves from the brussels sprouts. Make a small slit across the base of the stem. Put the sprouts in a large steamer and cover with a lid. Sit the steamer over a saucepan or wok of boiling water and steam for 15 minutes, or until tender. Refresh under cold water to stop the cooking process.

Put the butter, mustard and honey in a saucepan over low heat and stir to melt the butter. Add the sprouts and toss until well coated in the butter mixture and heated through. Pile onto a serving plate and serve immediately.

Serves 4

Quinoa with winter greens

200 g (7 oz/1 cup) quinoa
250 ml (9 fl oz/1 cup) chicken or
    vegetable stock
5 brussels sprouts, thickly sliced
100 g (3½ oz/2 cups) shredded
    cavolo nero or silverbeet (Swiss
    chard)
½ small red onion, finely sliced
25 g (1 oz/¼ cup) walnut halves,
    broken

Dressing
1½ tablespoons olive oil
1 tablespoon walnut oil
2 teaspoons balsamic vinegar
2 teaspoons dijon mustard
1 garlic clove, crushed

Put the quinoa in a bowl and cover with water. Leave for 2–3 minutes, then strain. Transfer to a large shallow saucepan which has a tight-fitting lid and lightly season with salt. Stir in the stock and scatter the brussels sprouts over the top.

Bring to the boil over medium heat then reduce the heat to low. Cover the pan with a sheet of foil, then the lid, and steam for 10–15 minutes. Add the cavolo nero and turn the quinoa over with a fork. Steam for a further 10 minutes, or until the sprouts are tender and the cavolo nero has wilted.

Meanwhile, to make the dressing, combine the olive oil, walnut oil, vinegar, mustard and garlic in a jar. Cover and shake well, then season to taste with salt and freshly ground black pepper.

Put onion and walnuts in a large bowl. Transfer the contents of the steamer to the bowl, add dressing and gently combine using a fork. This dish can be served warm or at room temperature.

Serves 4

Broad bean and pea pesto with broccolini

100 g (3½ oz/²/₃ cup) frozen peas
115 g (4 oz/³/₄ cup) frozen shelled
   broad (fava) beans
35 g (1¼ oz/¹/₃ cup) grated parmesan
   cheese
4 tablespoons finely chopped basil
1 garlic clove, crushed
2 teaspoons grated lemon zest
30 g (1 oz/¹/₄ cup) roughly chopped
   toasted pecans
4 tablespoons olive oil
425 g (15 oz) broccolini, washed and
   stems trimmed

Place the peas and broad beans in a steamer and cover with a lid. Sit the steamer over a saucepan or wok of boiling water and steam for 2 minutes, or until the peas and beans are only half cooked.

Strain the peas and beans into a colander, then refresh under cold running water. Drain well, then put them in a food processor. Add the parmesan, basil, garlic, lemon zest and salt and freshly ground black pepper, and pulse briefly so that the mixture isn't overly processed (it should be quite rough). Spoon the mixture into a large bowl, add the pecans and stir in the olive oil. Check the seasoning and add more salt and pepper if necessary.

Put broccolini in a steamer and cover with a lid. Steam for 5 minutes, or until the broccolini is a little under-cooked.

Stir 2 tablespoons of the steaming water into the pesto, then add the hot broccolini and carefully toss through. Serve immediately.

Serves 4

Asparagus bundles

190 g (6¾ oz/12 spears) asparagus
1 tablespoon extra virgin olive oil
1 tablespoon lemon juice
4 slices of prosciutto
60 g (2¼ oz/¼ cup) ricotta cheese
25 g (1 oz/¼ cup) grated parmesan
  cheese

Break the ends off the asparagus spears and cut the spears in half crossways. Place in a steamer and cover with a lid. Sit the steamer over a saucepan or wok of boiling water and steam for 5–7 minutes, or until tender.

Transfer the asparagus to a small bowl and toss with the olive oil, lemon juice and some salt and freshly ground black pepper. Wrap bundles of six asparagus pieces (three of each end) in each slice of prosciutto and place on a grill (broiler) tray.

Mix together the ricotta and parmesan and spread the mixture over the prosciutto. Place the tray under a preheated medium grill (broiler) for 10 minutes, or until the cheese starts to turn golden. Serve immediately.

Serves 4

Chickpeas and silverbeet

250 g (9 oz) dried chickpeas, soaked
  in water overnight
1 carrot, diced
1 sprig flat-leaf (Italian) parsley
1 bay leaf
2 brown onions, chopped
80 ml (2½ fl oz/⅓ cup) extra virgin
  olive oil
1 garlic clove, chopped
2 tomatoes, chopped
250 g (9 oz) silverbeet (Swiss chard),
  washed well and chopped
2 hard-boiled eggs, peeled and
  chopped

Drain and rinse the chickpeas and put
in a large saucepan with the carrot,
parsley, bay leaf and half the chopped
onion. Cover with 750 ml (26 fl oz/
3 cups) of water, bring to the boil and
cook for about 20 minutes, or until
almost tender. Add 2 teaspoons salt
and half the oil and cook for a further
10 minutes.

Heat the remaining oil in a frying pan
over medium heat and cook the
remaning onion and the garlic for
5 minutes, or until softened. Add the
tomato and cook for 5 minutes. Stir
the tomato mixture into the chickpea
mixture (it should be wet enough to be
saucy but not too soupy). Stir in the
silverbeet. Cook for 5 minutes, or until
silverbeet is tender. Season well and
serve garnished with the boiled egg.

Serves 4

Widowed potatoes

500 ml (17 fl oz/2 cups) extra virgin olive oil, for shallow frying
3 large all-purpose potatoes (such as desiree), cut into 1cm (½ in) slices
3 eggs, beaten
plain (all-purpose) flour for coating and thickening
4 garlic cloves, finely chopped
2 small brown onions, finely chopped
4 small tomatoes, peeled, seeded and finely chopped
1 teaspoon caster (superfine) sugar
400 ml (14 fl oz) beef stock

Preheat the oven to 160°C (315°F/ Gas 2–3). Heat the olive oil in a frying pan over medium–high heat.

Dip the potato slices in the beaten egg, then the flour. Fry for 2 minutes per side, or until golden on both sides. Transfer to a heatproof casserole or baking dish.

Add the garlic and onion to the frypan and cook for 5 minutes over medium heat or until softened, then add the chopped tomato and cook over a low heat until it reduces slightly. Add the sugar and stir to combine.

Sprinkle ½ teaspoon of flour over the mixture, stir through until it is smooth, then evenly pour over the potatoes. Gently pour over the stock and season with a little salt. Cover and cook in the 160°C oven for 45 minutes, then uncover and cook for a further 15 minutes or until the potatoes are tender.

Serves 4

Valencian peas

a pinch of saffron threads
2 tablespoons white wine
2 tablespoons olive oil
1 small onion, finely diced
1 garlic clove, crushed
¼ teaspoon ground cumin
125ml (4 fl oz/½ cup) chicken stock
1 bay leaf
310 g (11 oz/2 cups) fresh or frozen
  peas
2 tablespoons chopped flat-leaf
  (Italian) parsley

Soak the saffron in the wine for 10 minutes to help bring out the colour. Heat the olive oil in a saucepan over medium heat. Sauté the onion, garlic and cumin for 2–3 minutes, or until the onion is translucent. Add the saffron wine mixture, stock, bay leaf and peas. Season with salt and freshly ground black pepper.

Bring to the boil then reduce to a steady simmer. Cook, uncovered, for about 5 minutes or until the peas are cooked and the liquid has evaporated. Sprinkle with the chopped parsley and season to taste.

Serves 4

Baked radicchio

1 kg (2 lb 4 oz) radicchio
2 tablespoons olive oil
100 g (4 oz) bacon, thinly sliced

Preheat oven to 180°C (350°F/Gas 4). Remove outer leaves of the radicchio and split the heads into four wedges.

Heat the olive oil in a flameproof casserole dish large enough to fit all the radicchio in a single layer (but do not add radicchio yet). Add the bacon and cook over medium heat until the fat has just melted but the meat is not crisp. Add the radicchio and then turn it over to coat it well. Bake, covered, for 25–30 minutes, until tender when pierced with a knife, turning radicchio occasionally. Season and transfer to a warm dish with all the liquid. Serve immediately.

Serves 4

Capsicums stuffed with lamb and couscous

6 x 150–180 g (5½–6 oz) red or yellow
  capsicums (peppers)
140 g (5 oz/¾ cup) instant couscous
2½ tablespoons olive oil
1 onion, grated
2 garlic cloves, chopped
1 teaspoon ground cumin
2 teaspoons ground coriander
½ teaspoon ground allspice
a large pinch of chilli flakes (optional)
1 small handful chopped flat-leaf
  (Italian) parsley
1 small handful chopped mint
1 teaspoon finely grated lemon rind
250 g (9 oz) minced (ground) lamb
65 g (2½ oz/½ cup) chopped
  pistachio nuts
500 ml (17 fl oz/2 cups) tomato
  passata (puréed tomatoes)

Preheat the oven to 190°C (375°F/ Gas 5). Cut the tops off the capsicums and reserve. Discard the membranes and seeds from inside the capsicums.

Place the couscous in a large heatproof bowl. Pour 125 ml (4 fl oz/½ cup) boiling water over, then cover and leave to stand for 3–5 minutes, or until the water is absorbed. Stir in 1 tablespoon of the oil, using a fork to break up any lumps. Stir in the onion, garlic, spices, herbs and rind. Add the lamb and pistachios, then season well with sea salt and freshly ground black pepper. Mix thoroughly, using your hands.

Spoon the mixture into the capsicum cavities. Stand the capsicums in a baking dish in which they will all fit snugly. Place the reserved capsicum lids on top.

Combine the passata with 250 ml (9 fl oz/ 1 cup) water and pour into the baking dish, around the capsicums. Drizzle the remaining oil over the capsicums. Cover with foil and bake for 20 minutes, then remove the foil and bake for another 25 minutes, or until the filling is cooked and capsicums are tender. Serve hot or at room temperature with the passata sauce.

Serves 6

Tomato, eggplant and olive caponata

3 firm tomatoes
5 bulb spring onions (scallions), trimmed but not peeled
3 slender eggplants (aubergines), cut lengthways into 5 mm (1/4 inch) thick slices
2 red capsicums (peppers), quartered
50 g (1 3/4 oz/1/3 cup) pitted kalamata olives
1 tablespoon toasted pine nuts
3 tablespoons torn mint leaves
3 tablespoons olive oil
3 teaspoons white wine vinegar
1 teaspoon caster (superfine) sugar
1 garlic clove, crushed

Heat the grill (broiler) to high and line the tray with foil. Sit the tomatoes and onions on the rack of the grill tray and cook for about 10 minutes, turning often, until the tomato skins are charred in patches and start to split.

Remove the tomatoes from the heat and put the eggplant and capsicum on the rack, skin-side-up. Grill (broil) for about 8 minutes, or until well browned, turning the eggplant halfway through cooking. Remove all the vegetables from the grill and put the capsicum in a plastic bag to sweat.

Peel the tomatoes, cut them into 2 cm (3/4 inch) chunks and place in a colander to drain. Cut the eggplant into thick strips and put them in a bowl. When the capsicum is cool, peel off the skin, then cut the flesh into strips. Halve the onions from top to bottom, then give them a light squeeze so that the centre pops out. Add the capsicum and onion to the eggplant along with the olives, pine nuts and mint and gently stir together.

Put the oil, vinegar, sugar and garlic in a screw-top jar and shake to combine. Season liberally with salt and pepper and drizzle over the grilled vegetables. Add the drained tomato and toss lightly. Serve at room temperature.

Serves 4

Light &
Main Meals

Vegetable, feta and pesto parcels

30 g (1 oz) butter
2 garlic cloves, crushed
150 g (5½ oz/9 spears) asparagus, trimmed and chopped
1 carrot, cut into thin strips
1 zucchini (courgette), cut into thin strips
1 red capsicum (pepper), cut into thin strips
6 spring onions (scallions), thinly sliced on the diagonal
90 g (3¼ oz) mild feta cheese, crumbled
8 sheets filo pastry
60 g (2¼ oz) butter, melted
90 g (3¼ oz/⅓ cup) good-quality ready-made pesto
2 teaspoons sesame seed
tomato chutney, to serve

Preheat oven to 200°C (400°F/Gas 6). Heat butter in a large frying pan, then add the garlic and vegetables. Cook over medium heat for 3–4 minutes, or until just tender. Cool completely and fold in the feta. Divide the mixture into four equal portions.

Work with four sheets of pastry at a time, keeping the rest covered with a damp tea towel (dish towel). Brush each sheet with melted butter and lay them on top of one another. Cut in half widthways and spread 1 tablespoon of the pesto in the centre of each half, leaving a 2 cm (1 inch) border lengthways. Place one portion of the vegetable feta mixture on top of the pesto. Repeat the process with the remaining pastry, pesto and filling.

Brush the edges of filo with a little butter, tuck in the sides and fold over the ends to make four parcels. Place on a greased baking tray, seam side down, brush with the remaining butter and sprinkle with sesame seeds. Bake for 20–25 minutes, or until golden. Cut in half diagonally and serve hot with tomato chutney.

Serves 4

Mushroom and chicken risotto with olive and herb sprinkle

1.125 litres (40 fl oz/4½ cups) chicken
   stock
1 tablespoon olive oil
20 g (¾ oz) butter
2 leeks, white part only, finely sliced
1 garlic clove, crushed
400 g (14 oz/4½ cups) sliced Swiss
   brown mushrooms
330 g (11½ oz/1½ cups) arborio rice
350 g (12 oz) boneless, skinless
   chicken breasts, diced
1 large handful of baby English
   spinach leaves
65 g (2¼ oz/⅔ cup) finely grated
   parmesan cheese

Olive and herb sprinkle
110 g (3¾ oz/½ cup) green olives,
   pitted and finely sliced
1 small handful of basil, torn
1 small handful of flat-leaf (Italian)
   parsley, torn
1 tablespoon grated lemon rind

Extras
25 g (1 oz/¼ cup) shaved parmesan
   cheese.

Put all the ingredients for the olive and herb sprinkle in a small bowl. Mix together and set aside until ready to serve.

Bring stock to the boil in a saucepan, then keep hot over low heat.

Heat the olive oil and butter in a large heavy-based saucepan over medium heat. Add the leek and garlic and sauté for 2 minutes, or until the leek has softened. Add the mushrooms and cook for a further 2 minutes, or until softened.

Add the rice and stir using a wooden spoon until the grains are well coated. Add a ladleful of hot stock to the rice and stir until the liquid has been completely absorbed. Continue to add the stock, one ladleful at a time, stirring constantly until the rice absorbs the stock before adding more. Stir in the chicken with the last ladlefuls of stock and cook for 5 minutes, or until the rice is *al dente* and creamy and the chicken is cooked through.

Stir in the spinach and parmesan and divide among serving bowls. Serve scattered with shaved parmesan and the olive and herb sprinkle.

Serves 4

Sweet potato gnocchi with wilted greens

500 g (1 lb 2 oz) russet or sebago
  potatoes, chopped
250 g (9 oz) orange sweet potato,
  chopped
1 egg yolk
2 tablespoons milk
¼ teaspoon ground nutmeg
155 g (1¼ cups) plain (all-purpose)
  flour
1 tablespoon olive oil
4 bacon slices, thinly sliced
1 small onion, chopped
80 ml (2½ fl oz/⅓ cup) sweet sherry
500 g (1 lb 2 oz) English spinach
40 g (1½ oz) butter
2 tablespoons toasted pine nuts

Preheat the oven to hot 220°C (425°F/Gas 7). Bake the potato and sweet potato in a roasting tin for 40–60 minutes, or until soft. Cut in half and leave for 10 minutes. While still warm, press through a sieve into a large bowl. Add the egg yolk and milk, then the nutmeg, 125 g (4½ oz/1 cup) flour and 1¼ teaspoons salt, and mix well to combine.

Lightly knead the mixture until it is smooth, adding more flour if it gets sticky. Roll into 2 cm cylinders, then cut into 2 cm (¾ inch) diagonal lengths. Indent on one side with a fork.

Heat the oil in a large frying pan, add the bacon and onion, and cook over medium heat for 5 minutes, or until the onion is just golden. Add the sherry, stir well and cook for 2 minutes, or until reduced slightly. Add the spinach and cook, stirring, for 2 minutes, or until wilted, but still bright green. Stir in the butter and season. Keep warm.

Cook the gnocchi in boiling water in batches for 2–3 minutes, or until they rise to the surface. Drain and toss through the sauce. Scatter the pine nuts over the top.

Serves 4

Asparagus and pistachio risotto

1 litre (35 fl oz/4 cups) vegetable stock
250 ml (9 fl oz/1 cup) dry white wine
4 tablespoons extra virgin olive oil
1 red onion, finely chopped
440 g (15½ oz/2 cups) arborio rice
310 g (11 oz/20 spears) asparagus,
  trimmed and cut into short lengths
125 ml (4 fl oz/½ cup) pouring
  (whipping) cream
100 g (3½ oz/1 cup) grated parmesan
  cheese
40 g (1½ oz/½ cup) shelled pistachio
  nuts, toasted and roughly chopped

Heat the stock and wine in a large saucepan and keep at simmering point on the stove top.

Heat the oil in another large saucepan. Add the onion and cook over medium heat for 3 minutes, or until soft. Add the rice and stir for 1 minute, or until translucent.

Add 125 ml (4 fl oz/½ cup) hot stock, stirring constantly until the liquid is absorbed. Continue adding more stock, a little at a time, stirring constantly for 20–25 minutes, or until the rice is tender and creamy (you may not need to add all the stock, or you may not have quite enough and will need to add a little water as well—every risotto is different). Add the asparagus during the last 5 minutes of cooking.

Remove from the heat and leave for 2 minutes, then stir in the cream and parmesan and season well. Serve sprinkled with pistachios.

Serves 4–6

Bucatini with eggplant and mushrooms

2 tablespoons olive oil
250 g (9 oz) mushrooms, sliced
1 eggplant (aubergine), diced
2 garlic cloves, crushed
820 g (1 lb 13 oz) tinned chopped
  tomatoes
500 g (1 lb 2 oz) bucatini or spaghetti
1 large handful chopped parsley
  (optional)

Heat the oil in a saucepan and cook the mushrooms, eggplant and garlic, stirring, for 4 minutes. Add the tomato, cover and simmer for 15 minutes.

Meanwhile, cook the pasta in a large saucepan of rapidly boiling salted water until al dente. Drain well and return to the pan to keep warm. Season the sauce with salt and freshly ground black pepper and stir in the parsley, if you wish. Toss with the pasta and serve immediately.

Serves 4–6

Hint: If the pasta is cooked before you are ready to serve you can prevent it sticking together by tossing it with a little olive oil after draining.

Frittata of zucchini flowers, oregano and ricotta salata

2 tablespoons olive oil
1 onion, finely chopped
2 garlic cloves, finely sliced
8 small zucchini (courgettes) with flowers
8 eggs, lightly whisked
4 tablespoons oregano, chopped
35 g (1¼ oz/⅓ cup) ricotta salata, grated (see Note)
25 g (1 oz/¼ cup) grated parmesan cheese
1 tablespoon shaved parmesan cheese
lemon wedges, to serve

Preheat the oven to 200°C (400°F/ Gas 6). Heat the oil in an ovenproof 20 cm (8 inch) frying pan and cook the onion and garlic until softened. Arrange the zucchini flowers evenly in the pan, and add the egg. Sprinkle the oregano, ricotta salata and grated parmesan over the top and season well with freshly ground black pepper.

Put the pan in the oven and cook for about 10 minutes, or until set. Remove from the oven and allow to cool slightly. Top with the shaved parmesan, cut into wedges and serve with a piece of lemon.

Serves 4

Note: Originating in Sicily, ricotta salata is a firm white rindless cheese with a nutty, sweet milky flavour. If unavailable, substitute with a mild feta cheese.

Beetroot ravioli with sage burnt butter

340 g (11¾ oz) jar baby beetroots
(beets) in sweet vinegar
40 g (1½ oz) grated parmesan
cheese
250 g (9 oz/1 cup) ricotta cheese
750 g (1 lb 10 oz) fresh lasagne sheets
fine cornmeal, for sprinkling
200 g (7 oz) salted butter, chopped
8 sage leaves, torn
2 garlic cloves, crushed

Drain the beetroot, then grate it into a bowl. Add the parmesan cheese and ricotta and mix well. Lay a sheet of pasta on a flat surface and place evenly spaced tablespoons of the beetroot mixture on the pasta to give 12 mounds—four across and three down. Flatten the mounds slightly. Lightly brush the edges of the pasta sheet and around each pile of filling with water.

Place a second sheet of pasta over the top and gently press around each mound to seal and enclose the filling. Using a fluted pastry cutter or sharp knife, cut the pasta into 12 ravioli. Lay them out separately on a lined tray that has been sprinkled with the cornmeal. Repeat with the remaining filling and lasagne sheets to make 24 ravioli. Gently remove any excess air bubbles after cutting so that they are completely sealed.

Cook the pasta in a large saucepan of rapidly boiling salted water until *al dente*. Drain well and return to the pan to keep warm. Melt the butter in a saucepan and cook for 3–4 minutes, or until golden brown. Remove from the heat, stir in the sage and garlic and spoon over the ravioli. Sprinkle with shaved parmesan to serve.

Serves 4

Fresh vegetable lasagne with rocket

Balsamic syrup
4 tablespoons balsamic vinegar
1½ tablespoons brown sugar

155 g (5½ oz/1 cup) fresh or frozen
  peas
250 g (9 oz/16 spears) asparagus,
  trimmed and cut into short lengths
2 large zucchini (courgettes), cut into
  thin ribbons
2 fresh lasagne sheets (each sheet
  24 x 35 cm/9½ x 14 inches)
100 g (3½ oz) rocket (arugula) leaves
1 very large handful basil, torn
2 tablespoons extra virgin olive oil
250 g (9 oz/1 cup) low-fat ricotta
  cheese
150 g (5½ oz) semi-dried (sun-
  blushed) tomatoes
parmesan cheese shaved, to serve

To make the syrup, place the vinegar
and sugar in a saucepan and stir over
medium heat until the sugar dissolves.
Reduce the heat and simmer for
4 minutes, or until the sauce becomes
syrupy. Remove from the heat.

Bring a pan of salted water to the
boil. Blanch the peas, asparagus and
zucchini in separate batches until
tender. Remove each batch with a
slotted spoon. Refresh in cold water.
Reserve the liquid. Return to the boil.

Cook the lasagne in the boiling water
for 1–2 minutes, or until *al dente*.
Refresh in cold water and drain well.
Cut each sheet in half lengthways.
Toss the vegetables and the rocket
with the basil and olive oil. Season.

To assemble, place one strip of pasta
on a plate—one-third on the centre
and two-thirds overhanging one side.
Place a small amount of the salad on
the centre one-third, topped with some
ricotta and tomato. Season and fold
over one-third of the sheet. Top with
another layer of salad, ricotta and
tomato. Fold back the final layer of
pasta and garnish with a little salad
and tomato. Repeat with the remaining
strips, salad, ricotta and tomato to
make four servings. Drizzle with the
syrup and sprinkle with parmesan.

Serves 4

Green curry with sweet potato and eggplant

1 tablespoon oil
1 onion, chopped
1–2 tablespoons green curry paste
  (see Note)
1 medium eggplant (aubergine),
  quartered and sliced
400 ml (14 fl oz) tinned coconut milk
250 ml (9 fl oz/1 cup) vegetable stock
6 makrut (kaffir) lime leaves
1 orange sweet potato, cut into cubes
2 teaspoons soft brown sugar
2 tablespoons lime juice
2 teaspoons lime zest
coriander (cilantro) leaves, to garnish

Heat the oil in a large wok or frying pan. Add the onion and curry paste and cook, stirring, over medium heat for 3 minutes. Add the eggplant and cook for a further 4–5 minutes, or until softened. Pour in the coconut milk and stock, bring to the boil, then reduce the heat and simmer for 5 minutes. Add the lime leaves and sweet potato and cook, stirring occasionally, for 10 minutes, or until the vegetables are very tender.

Mix in the sugar, lime juice and lime zest until well combined with the vegetables. Season to taste with salt. Garnish with coriander leaves and serve with steamed rice.

Serves 4–6

Note: If this is to be a vegetarian meal, make sure you choose a green curry paste that does not contain shrimp paste.

Mushroom moussaka

1 eggplant (aubergine), cut into 1 cm (½ inch) slices
1 large potato, cut into 1 cm (½ inch) slices
30 g (1 oz) butter
1 onion, finely chopped
2 garlic cloves, finely chopped
500 g (1 lb 2 oz) flat mushrooms, sliced
400 g (14 oz) tinned chopped tomatoes
½ teaspoon sugar
40 g (1½ oz) butter, extra
40 g (1½ oz/⅓ cup) plain (all-purpose) flour
500 ml (17 fl oz/2 cups) milk
1 egg, lightly beaten
40 g (1½ oz) grated parmesan cheese

Preheat the oven to 220°C (425°F/ Gas 7). Line a large baking tray with foil and brush with oil. Put the eggplant and potato in a single layer on the tray and sprinkle with salt and pepper. Bake for 20 minutes.

Melt the butter in a pan over medium heat. Add the onion and cook, stirring, for 3–4 minutes, or until soft. Add the garlic and cook for 1 minute. Turn the heat to high, add the mushrooms and stir continuously for 2–3 minutes, or until soft. Add the tomato, reduce the heat and simmer rapidly for 8 minutes, or until reduced. Stir in the sugar.

Melt the extra butter in a pan over low heat. Add the flour and cook for 1 minute. Remove from the heat. Slowly stir in the milk. Return to the heat and stir until it boils. Reduce the heat and simmer for 2 minutes. Remove from the heat. When the bubbles ebb, stir in the egg and parmesan.

Reduce the oven to 180°C (350°F/ Gas 4). Grease a 1.5 litre (52 fl oz/ 6 cup) ovenproof dish. Spoon one-third of the mixture in and cover with potato. Top with half the mushrooms, then the eggplant. Finish with the remaining mushrooms, pour on the sauce. Bake for 30–35 minutes. Leave for 10 minutes before serving.

Serves 4–6

Spicy broccoli and cauliflower stir-fry

1 teaspoon ground cumin
1 teaspoon ground coriander
2 tablespoons oil
2 garlic cloves, crushed
1 teaspoon grated fresh ginger
1/2 teaspoon chilli powder
1 onion, cut into wedges
200 g (7 oz) cauliflower, cut into bite-
 sized florets
200 g (7 oz) broccoli, cut into bite-
 sized florets
200 g (7 oz) haloumi cheese, diced
1 tablespoon lemon juice

Heat the wok until very hot, add the cumin and coriander, and dry-fry the spices for 1 minute. Add the oil with the garlic, ginger and chilli powder, and stir-fry briefly. Add the onion and cook for 2–3 minutes, being careful not to burn the spices.

Add the cauliflower and broccoli, and stir-fry until they are cooked through but still crisp. Add the haloumi and toss well until the haloumi is coated with the spices and is just beginning to melt. Season well. Serve sprinkled generously with lemon juice.

Serves 4

Chicken, broccoli and pasta bake

300 g (10½ oz) pasta
425 g (15 oz) tinned cream of
  mushroom soup
2 eggs
185 g (6½ oz/¾ cup) mayonnaise
1 tablespoon dijon mustard
200 g (7 oz) grated cheddar cheese
600 g (1 lb 5 oz) boneless, skinless
  chicken breasts, thinly sliced
400 g (14 oz) frozen broccoli pieces,
  thawed
40 g (1½ oz/½ cup) fresh
  breadcrumbs

Preheat the oven to 180°C (350°F/ Gas 4). Cook the pasta in a large saucepan of rapidly boiling salted water until *al dente*. Drain well and return to the pan to keep warm. Combine the soup, eggs, mayonnaise, mustard and half the cheese in a bowl.

Heat a lightly greased non-stick frying pan over medium heat, add the chicken and cook for 5–6 minutes, or until cooked through. Season with salt and freshly ground black pepper, then set aside to cool.

Add the chicken and broccoli to the pasta. Pour the soup mixture over the top and stir. Transfer the mixture to a 3 litre (105 fl oz/12 cup) ovenproof dish. Sprinkle with combined breadcrumbs and remaining cheese. Bake for 20 minutes, or until it becomes golden brown.

Serves 6–8

Mushroom pot pies

5 tablespoons olive oil
1 leek, sliced
1 garlic clove, crushed
1 kg (2 lb 4 oz) large field mushrooms,
  roughly chopped
1 teaspoon chopped thyme
300 ml (10½ fl oz) pouring (whipping)
  cream
1 sheet ready-rolled puff pastry,
  thawed
1 egg yolk, beaten, to glaze

Preheat the oven to 180°C (350°F/ Gas 4). Heat 1 tablespoon of the oil in a frying pan over medium heat. Cook the leek and garlic for 5 minutes, or until the leek is soft and translucent. Transfer to a large saucepan.

Heat the remaining oil in the frying pan over high heat and cook the mushrooms in two batches, stirring frequently, for 5–7 minutes per batch, or until the mushrooms have released their juices and are soft and slightly coloured. Transfer to the saucepan, then add the thyme.

Place the saucepan over high heat and stir in the cream. Cook, stirring occasionally, for 7–8 minutes, or until the cream has reduced to a thick sauce. Remove from the heat and season well with salt and freshly ground black pepper.

Divide the filling among four 310 ml (10¾ fl oz/1¼ cup) ramekins or ovenproof bowls. Cut the pastry into rounds slightly larger than each dish. Brush the rim of the ramekins with a little of the egg yolk, place the pastry on top and press down to seal. Brush the top with the remaining egg yolk. Place the ramekins on a metal tray. Bake for 20–25 minutes, or until the pastry has risen and is golden brown.

Serves 4

Green stir-fry with sesame and soy

2 tablespoons light soy sauce
1 tablespoon hoisin sauce
1 tablespoon vegetable or chicken
  stock
2 tablespoons vegetable oil
1 teaspoon sesame oil
4 garlic cloves, finely sliced
2 teaspoons ginger, cut into thin strips
2 kg (4 lb 8 oz/4 bunches) baby bok
  choy (pak choi), cut into quarters,
  well washed and drained
200 g (7 oz) snowpeas (mangetout),
  trimmed
200 g (7 oz) sugar snap peas,
  trimmed
2 tablespoons bamboo shoots, cut
  into thin strips
jasmine rice, to serve

In a small bowl mix together the light soy sauce, hoisin sauce and stock.

Heat a wok over high heat and add the vegetable and sesame oils. Stir-fry the garlic, ginger and bok choy for 3 minutes. Add the snowpeas, sugar snap peas and bamboo shoots and stir-fry for a further 5 minutes. Pour in the sauce, and gently toss until the sauce has reduced slightly to coat the just tender vegetables. Serve immediately with jasmine rice.

Serves 4

Vegetable casserole with herb dumplings

1 tablespoon olive oil
1 large onion, chopped
2 garlic cloves, crushed
2 teaspoons sweet paprika
1 large potato, chopped
1 large carrot, sliced
400 g (14 oz) tinned chopped
 tomatoes
375 ml (13 fl oz/1½ cups) vegetable
 stock
400 g (14 oz) orange sweet potato,
 cubed
150 g (5½ oz) broccoli, cut into florets
2 zucchini (courgettes), thickly sliced
125 g (4½ oz/1 cup) self-raising flour
20 g (¾ oz) cold butter, cut into small
 cubes
2 teaspoons chopped parsley
1 teaspoon thyme
1 teaspoon chopped rosemary
4 tablespoons milk
2 tablespoons light sour cream

Heat the oil in a large saucepan and add the onion. Cook over low heat, stirring occasionally, for 5 minutes, or until soft. Add the garlic and paprika and cook, stirring, for 1 minute.

Add the potato, carrot, tomato and stock to the pan. Bring to the boil, then reduce the heat and simmer, covered, for 10 minutes. Add the potato, broccoli, zucchini and simmer for 10 minutes, or until tender. Preheat the oven to 200°C (400°F/Gas 6).

To make the dumplings, sift the flour and a pinch of salt into a bowl and add the butter. Rub the butter into the flour with your fingertips until it resembles fine breadcrumbs. Stir in the herbs and make a well in the centre. Add the milk, and mix with a flat-bladed knife, using a cutting action, until the mixture comes together in beads. Gather up the dough and lift onto a lightly floured surface. Divide into eight portions. Shape each portion into a ball.

Add the sour cream to the casserole. Pour into a 2 litre (70 fl oz/8 cup) ovenproof dish and top with the dumplings. Bake for 20 minutes, or until the dumplings are golden and a skewer comes out clean when inserted in the centre.

Serves 4

Orechiette with anchovies, broccoli and basil

600 g (1 lb 5 oz) broccoli, cut into
  florets
500 g (1 lb 2 oz) orecchiette
1 tablespoon olive oil
4 garlic cloves, finely chopped
8 anchovy fillets, roughly chopped
250 ml (9 fl oz/1 cup) pouring
  (whipping) cream
2 large handfuls basil, torn
2 teaspoons finely grated lemon zest
100 g (3½ oz/1 cup) parmesan
  cheese, grated

Blanch the broccoli in a large saucepan of boiling salted water for 3–4 minutes. Remove and plunge into chilled water. Drain well with a slotted spoon.

Cook the pasta in a large saucepan of rapidly boiling salted water until *al dente*. Drain well and return to the pan to keep warm, reserving 2 tablespoons of the cooking water.

Meanwhile, heat the oil in a frying pan over medium heat. Add the garlic and anchovy and cook for 1–2 minutes, or until the garlic begins to turn golden. Add the broccoli and cook for a further 5 minutes. Add the cream and half the basil and cook for 10 minutes, or until the cream has reduced and slightly thickened and the broccoli is very tender.

Purée half the mixture in a food processor until nearly smooth, then return to the pan with the lemon zest, half the parmesan and the reserved cooking water. Stir together well, then season. Add the warm pasta and remaining basil, and toss until well combined. Sprinkle with the remaining parmesan and serve immediately.

Serves 4–6

Asparagus pie

800 g (1 lb 12 oz) asparagus
20 g (¾ oz) butter
½ teaspoon chopped thyme
1 French shallot, chopped
1 large sheet ready-rolled shortcrust
  pastry
80 ml (2½ fl oz/⅓ cup) pouring
  (whipping) cream
2 tablespoons grated parmesan
  cheese
1 egg
pinch ground nutmeg
1 egg, extra, lightly beaten

Trim the asparagus spears to 10 cm (4 inches) and cut thick spears in half lengthways. Heat the butter in a large frying pan over medium heat and add the asparagus, thyme and shallot. Add a tablespoon of water and season with salt and freshly ground black pepper. Cook, stirring, for 3 minutes, or until the asparagus is tender.

Preheat the oven to 200°C (400°F/ Gas 6) and grease a 21 cm (8½ inch) fluted, loose-based flan (tart) tin. Roll the pastry out to a 2 mm (⅛ inch) thick circle with a diameter of about 30 cm (12 inches). Line the flan tin and trim the pastry using kitchen scissors, leaving about 8 cm (3 inches) above the top of the tin. Arrange half the asparagus in one direction across the bottom of the dish. Cover with the remaining asparagus, running in the opposite direction.

Combine the cream, parmesan, egg and nutmeg and season. Pour over the asparagus. Fold the pastry over the filling, forming loose pleats. Brush with beaten egg and bake in the centre of the oven for 25 minutes, or until golden.

Serves 6

Spinach and zucchini frittata

1 tablespoon olive oil
1 red onion, thinly sliced
2 zucchini (courgettes), sliced
1 garlic clove, crushed
300 g (10½ oz) baby English spinach
  leaves, stalks removed
6 eggs
2 tablespoons pouring (whipping)
  cream
80 g (3 oz) emmenthal cheese, grated

Heat the oil in a medium non-stick frying pan and fry the onion and zucchini over medium heat until they are a pale golden brown. Add the garlic and cook it for a minute. Add the spinach and cook until the spinach has wilted and any excess moisture has evaporated off — if you don't do this, your frittata will end up soggy in the middle, as the liquid will continue to come out as it cooks. Shake the pan so you get an even layer of mixture. Turn the heat down to low.

Beat the eggs and cream together and season with salt and freshly ground black pepper. Stir in half of the cheese and pour the mixture over the spinach. Cook the bottom of the frittata for about 4 minutes, or until the egg is just set. While you are doing this, turn on the grill (broiler). When the bottom of the frittata is set, scatter on the rest of the cheese and put the frying pan under the grill to cook the top.

Turn the frittata out of the frying pan after leaving it to set for a minute. Cut it into wedges to serve.

Serves 4

Eggplant parmigiana

3 tablespoons olive oil, plus extra, for
  shallow-frying
1 onion, diced
2 garlic cloves, crushed
1.25 kg (2 lb 12 oz) tomatoes, peeled
  and chopped
1 kg (2 lb 4 oz) eggplants (aubergines)
250 g (9 oz) bocconcini (fresh baby
  mozzarella cheese), sliced
185 g (6½ oz) cheddar cheese, finely
  grated
2 large handfuls basil leaves
50 g (1¾ oz/½ cup) grated parmesan

Heat the oil in a large frying pan, add
the onion and cook over moderate
heat until soft. Add the garlic and cook
for 1 minute. Add the tomato and
simmer for 15 minutes. Season with
salt to taste. Set aside and keep
warm. Preheat the oven to 200°C
(400°F/Gas 6).

Slice the eggplants very thinly and
shallow-fry in a separate frying pan in
oil in batches for 3–4 minutes, or until
golden brown. Drain on paper towels.

Place one-third of the eggplant in a
1.75 litre (60 fl oz/7 cup) ovenproof
dish. Top with half the bocconcini and
cheddar. Repeat the layers, finishing
with a layer of eggplant.

Pour the tomato mixture over the
eggplant. Scatter with torn basil
leaves, then parmesan. Bake for
40 minutes.

Serves 6–8

Variation: If you prefer not to fry the
eggplant, brush it lightly with oil and
brown lightly under a hot grill (broiler).

Stuffed eggplants

60 g (2¼ oz/⅓ cup) brown lentils
2 large eggplants (aubergines)
cooking oil spray
1 red onion, chopped
2 garlic cloves, crushed
1 red capsicum (pepper), finely
   chopped
40 g (1½ oz/¼ cup) pine nuts, toasted
140 g (5 oz/¾ cup) cooked short-
   grain rice
440 g (15½ oz) tinned chopped
   tomatoes
2 tablespoons chopped coriander
   (cilantro)
1 tablespoon chopped parsley
2 tablespoons grated parmesan
   cheese

Simmer the brown lentils in a saucepan of water for 25 minutes, or until soft; drain. Slice the eggplants in half lengthways and scoop out the flesh, leaving a 1 cm (½ inch) shell. Chop the flesh finely.

Spray a large, deep non-stick frying pan with oil, add 1 tablespoon water to the pan, then add the onion and garlic and stir until softened. Add the cooked lentils to the pan with the capsicum, pine nuts, rice, tomato and eggplant flesh. Stir over medium heat for 10 minutes, or until the eggplant has softened. Add the coriander and parsley. Season, then toss until well mixed.

Cook the eggplant shells in boiling water for 4–5 minutes, or until tender. Spoon the filling into the eggplant shells and sprinkle with the parmesan. Grill (broil) for 5–10 minutes, or until golden. Serve immediately.

Serves 4

Thai basil fried rice

2 tablespoons oil
3 Asian shallots, sliced
1 garlic clove, finely chopped
1 small red chilli, finely chopped
100 g (3½ oz) snake (yard-long) or
    green beans, cut into short pieces
1 small red capsicum (pepper), cut
    into batons
90 g (3¼ oz) button mushrooms,
    halved
470 g (2½ cups) cooked jasmine rice
1 teaspoon grated palm sugar (jiggery)
3 tablespoons light soy sauce
3 tablespoons fresh Thai basil,
    shredded
1 tablespoon coriander (cilantro)
    leaves, chopped
fried red Asian shallot flakes, to
    garnish
Thai basil leaves, to garnish

Heat a wok over high heat, add
the oil and swirl. Stir-fry the shallots,
garlic and chilli for 3 minutes, or until
the shallots brown. Add the beans,
capsicum and mushrooms, stir-fry
for 3 minutes, or until cooked, then
stir in the cooked jasmine rice and
heat through.

Dissolve the palm sugar in the soy
sauce, then pour over the rice. Stir in
the herbs. Garnish with the shallot
flakes and basil.

Serves 4

Roast vegetables with poached egg and camembert

12 baby onions or French shallots
80 ml (2½ fl oz/⅓ cup) olive oil
350 g (12 oz/22 spears) asparagus,
    cut into 4 cm (1½ inch) pieces
4 zucchini (courgettes), thickly sliced
2 eggplants (aubergines), cubed
8 garlic cloves
2 tablespoons lemon juice
4 eggs
250 g (9 oz) camembert cheese,
    cubed

Turn the oven on to 200 C (400 F/ Gas 6). Peel the baby onions, leaving them still attached at the root end. Don't leave any root on.

Put the oil in a roasting tin and add the onions, asparagus, zucchini and eggplant, along with the garlic, and toss well. Season with salt and freshly ground black pepper. Put the tin in the oven and roast the vegetables for 20 minutes. Sprinkle on the lemon juice and roast for another 10 minutes.

Put a large frying pan full of water over a high heat and bring to the boil. When the water is bubbling, turn the heat down to a gentle simmer. Crack an egg into a cup and slip the egg into the water – it should start to turn opaque. Do the same with the other egg, keeping them separate. Turn the heat down as low as you can and leave the eggs for 3 minutes.

Divide the vegetables between four ovenproof dishes. Put the camembert on top of the vegetables, dividing it among the dishes. Put the dishes back in the oven for a couple of minutes to start the cheese melting.

Top each dish with a poached egg and some freshly ground black pepper.

Serves 4

Roasted pumpkin and spinach quiche

500 g (1 lb 2 oz) butternut pumpkin
  (squash)
1 red onion, cut into small wedges
2 tablespoons olive oil
1 garlic clove, crushed
4 eggs
125 ml (4 fl oz/½ cup) pouring
  (whipping) cream
125 ml (4 fl oz/½ cup) milk
1 tablespoon chopped parsley
1 tablespoon chopped coriander
  (cilantro)
1 teaspoon wholegrain mustard
6 sheets filo pastry
50 g (1¾ oz) English spinach,
  blanched
1 tablespoon grated parmesan cheese

Preheat the oven to 190°C (375°F/ Gas 5). Slice the pumpkin into 1 cm (½ inch) pieces, leaving the skin on. Place the pumpkin, onion, 1 tablespoon of the olive oil, garlic and 1 teaspoon of salt in a roasting tin. Roast for 1 hour, or until lightly golden and cooked.

Whisk together the eggs, cream, milk, herbs and mustard. Season with salt and freshly ground black pepper.

Grease a loose-based fluted flan (tart) tin or ovenproof dish measuring 22 cm (8½ inches) across the base. Brush each sheet of filo pastry with oil and then line the flan tin with the six sheets. Fold the sides down, tucking them into the tin to form a crust.

Heat a baking tray in the oven for 10 minutes. Place the flan tin on the tray and arrange all the vegetables over the base. Pour the egg mixture over the vegetables and sprinkle with the parmesan.

Bake for 35–40 minutes, or until the filling is golden brown and set.

Serves 4–6

Polenta pie

2 eggplants (aubergines), thickly sliced
330 ml (11¼ fl oz/1⅓ cups) vegetable
  stock
150 g (5½ oz/1 cup) fine polenta
60 g (2¼ oz/heaped ½ cup) finely
  grated parmesan cheese
1 tablespoon olive oil
1 large onion, chopped
2 garlic cloves, crushed
1 large red capsicum (pepper), diced
2 zucchini (courgettes), thickly sliced
150 g (5½ oz) button mushrooms, cut
  into quarters
400 g (14 oz) tinned chopped
  tomatoes
3 teaspoons balsamic vinegar
olive oil, for brushing

Spread the eggplant in a single layer on a board and sprinkle with salt. Leave for 15 minutes, then rinse, pat dry and cut into cubes.

Line a 23 cm (9 inch) round cake tin with foil. Pour the stock and 330 ml (11¼ fl oz/1⅓ cups) water into a pan. Bring to the boil. Add the polenta in a thin stream and stir over low heat until the liquid is absorbed. Remove from the heat and stir in the cheese until it melts. Spread into the tin, smoothing the surface as much as possible. Refrigerate until set.

Preheat the oven to 200°C (400°F/ Gas 6). Heat the oil in a pan with a lid and add the onion. Cook over medium heat, stirring occasionally, for about 3 minutes. Add the garlic and cook for a further minute. Add the vegetables and tomato. Bring to the boil, then reduce the heat and simmer, covered, for about 20 minutes. Stir to prevent it sticking. Stir in the vinegar.

Transfer the mixture to a 23 cm (9 inch) ovenproof pie dish. Turn out the polenta, peel off the foil and cut into 12 wedges. Arrange smooth side down in a single layer, over the vegetables. Brush lightly with a little olive oil and bake for 20 minutes, or until lightly brown and crisp.

Serves 6

Peppered pork, zucchini and garganelli

450 g pork fillet
3–4 teaspoons cracked black
  peppercorns
80 g (2¾ oz) butter
250 g (9 oz) garganelli pasta
1 onion, halved and thinly sliced
2 large zucchini (courgettes), thinly
  sliced
1 large handful basil, torn
155 g (¾ cup) baby black olives
60 g (2¼ oz/½ cup) grated romano
  cheese

Cut the pork fillet in half widthways and roll in the pepper and some salt. Heat half the butter in a large deep frying pan, add the pork and cook for 4 minutes on each side, or until golden brown and just cooked through. Remove from the pan and cut into 5 mm (2 inch) slices, then set aside and keep warm.

Cook the pasta in a large saucepan of boiling water until *al dente*; drain well and return to the pan.

Meanwhile, melt remaining butter in the frying pan, add the onion and cook, stirring, over medium heat for about 3 minutes, or until soft. Add the zucchini and toss for 5 minutes, or until starting to soften. Add the basil, olives, sliced pork and any juices and toss well. Stir the pork mixture through the hot pasta, then season to taste with salt and cracked black pepper. Serve immediately topped with cheese.

Serves 4

Veal tortellini with creamy mushroom sauce

500 g (1 lb 2 oz) veal tortellini
60 ml (2 fl oz/¼ cup) olive oil
600 g (1 lb 5 oz) Swiss brown
  mushrooms, thinly sliced
2 cloves garlic, crushed
125 ml (4 fl oz/½ cup) dry white wine
300 ml (10½ fl oz) thick (double/heavy)
  cream
pinch ground nutmeg
3 tablespoons finely chopped flat-leaf
  (Italian) parsley
30 g (1 oz) grated parmesan cheese

Cook the pasta in a large saucepan of boiling water until *al dente*. Drain. Meanwhile, heat the oil in a frying pan over medium heat. Add the mushrooms and cook, stirring occasionally, for 5 minutes, or until softened. Add the garlic and cook for 1 minute, then stir in the wine and cook for 5 minutes, or until the liquid has reduced by half.

Combine the cream, nutmeg and parsley, add to the sauce and cook for 3–5 minutes, or until the sauce thickens slightly. Season. Divide the tortellini among four serving plates and spoon on the mushroom sauce. Sprinkle with the parmesan and serve.

Serves 4

Roast chicken and vegetables with salsa verde

300 g (10½ oz) pumpkin (winter squash), peeled, seeded and cut into 2.5 cm (1 inch) chunks
300 g (10½ oz) orange sweet potato, peeled and cut into 3 cm (1¼ inch) chunks
10 small roasting potatoes, halved
2 red onions, each cut into 8 wedges
2 tablespoons olive oil
1.6 kg (3 lb 8 oz) free-range chicken
1 lemon, quartered
3 garlic cloves, peeled
1 tablespoon plain (all-purpose) flour
250 ml (9 fl oz/1 cup) chicken stock
310 g (11 oz/2 cups) frozen peas

Salsa verde
2 garlic cloves, peeled
1 tablespoon small capers, rinsed and drained
4 anchovy fillets, drained
2 large handfuls of parsley
1 large handful of mint
1 tablespoon lemon juice
1 tablespoon dijon mustard
60 ml (2 fl oz/¼ cup) extra virgin olive oil

Preheat the oven to 180°C (350°F/ Gas 4). Toss the pumpkin, sweet potato, potatoes and onion in a bowl with half the olive oil. Season well.

Rinse the chicken. Pat dry with paper towels. Put the lemon and garlic inside the chicken. Rub the remaining oil over the skin and season with pepper. Place in a flameproof roasting tin and arrange the vegetables around. Roast for 1 hour, or until the juices run clear from the chicken when skewered.

Transfer the chicken and vegetables to a large platter and cover with foil to keep warm. Heat the roasting tin on the stovetop over medium heat. Stir in the flour, scraping up any bits stuck to the base, and cook for 1–2 minutes, stirring constantly. Gradually add the stock, stirring constantly to prevent lumps forming, then bring to the boil. Cook, stirring, for 4–5 minutes, or until the gravy has boiled and thickened.

Meanwhile, bring a small saucepan of water to the boil and add the peas. Cook for 2–3 minutes, then drain well.

Put all the salsa verde ingredients in a food processor and blend to a coarse paste. Season with pepper. Carve the chicken and serve with the peas, vegetables and the salsa verde.

Serves 4

Rice noodle, beef and vegetable stir-fry

150 g (5½ oz) rump or skirt steak, trimmed and finely sliced
2 teaspoons cornflour (cornstarch)
2 teaspoons oyster sauce
1½ tablespoons soy sauce
1 garlic clove, chopped
2 tablespoons vegetable oil
1 carrot, cut into thin strips
1 small red capsicum (pepper), sliced
3 baby bok choy (pak choy), sliced into 2.5 cm (1 inch) chunks
500 g (1 lb 2 oz) fresh rice noodles (available from the Asian section in supermarkets or Asian food stores)
100 g (3½ oz/1 cup) bean sprouts, tails trimmed

Extras
chopped red chilli, to serve
coriander (cilantro) leaves, to serve

Put the steak in a bowl with the cornflour, oyster sauce, 1 teaspoon of the soy sauce and the garlic. Stir to coat well.

In a wok or large non-stick frying pan, heat 1 tablespoon of the oil over medium–high heat. Stir-fry the meat for 1–2 minutes, or until golden and cooked through. Remove from the wok and set aside.

Wipe the wok clean, then heat the remaining oil over medium–high heat. Add the carrot and capsicum and cook for 1–2 minutes, then add the bok choy and cook for another minute, or until it begins to wilt. Add the noodles, beef mixture and remaining soy sauce and cook, tossing, for 5–6 minutes, or until the noodles soften and the ingredients are well combined.

Toss the bean sprouts through, then remove from the heat and leave to stand for 1–2 minutes before serving.

Serve the noodles sprinkled with chilli and coriander.

Serves 4

Roast lamb with summer vegetables

1.5 kg (3 lb 5 oz) boneless leg of lamb
1 tablespoon capers, drained and roughly chopped
1 large handful parsley, finely chopped
6 anchovy fillets, chopped
2 garlic cloves, crushed
3 teaspoons lemon juice
½ teaspoon finely grated lemon rind
1 tablespoon olive oil

Summer vegetables
1 red onion, cut into 2 cm (¾ inch) chunks
1 red capsicum (pepper), cut into 3 cm (1¼ inch) pieces
12 garlic cloves, peeled
1 eggplant (aubergine), cut into 2 cm (¾ inch) chunks
2 zucchini (courgettes), cut in half lengthways, then sliced
500 g (1 lb 2 oz) cherry tomatoes, halved
60 ml (2 fl oz/¼ cup) olive oil
1 small handful mint
50 g (1¾ oz/½ cup) shaved parmesan cheese

Preheat the oven to 180°C (350°F/ Gas 4). Remove any string or netting from the lamb, then open up, skin side down, on a chopping board. In a bowl mix together the capers, parsley, anchovies, garlic, juice, rind and oil. Spread the mixture over the lamb, reserving the bowl, then roll the lamb up and tie at 2 cm (¾ inch) intervals with kitchen string to keep it in shape.

Place the lamb in a roasting tin and season with sea salt and ground black pepper. Roast for 30 minutes.

Meanwhile, start preparing the summer vegetables. Put the onion, capsicum, garlic, eggplant, zucchini, tomatoes and olive oil in the reserved bowl. Season and toss to combine.

Add the vegetable mixture to the roasting tin and bake for 45 minutes, or until the lamb is cooked to your liking and the vegetables are soft.

Remove the lamb to a plate, cover loosely with foil and allow to rest for 15 minutes. Meanwhile, roast the vegetables for a further 10 minutes, or until tender. Transfer the vegetables to a serving bowl and scatter with the mint and shaved parmesan. Carve the lamb in slices and serve with the summer vegetables.

Serves 6

Pork schnitzels with warm roasted beetroot and potato salad

500 g (1 lb 2 oz) pork fillet, trimmed
   and cut into 8 equal portions
115 g (4 oz/2 cups) panko (Japanese
   breadcrumbs)
2 teaspoons dried oregano
1 teaspoon dried mint
1 handful flat-leaf (Italian) parsley,
   chopped
2 teaspoons finely grated lemon rind
150 g (5½ oz/1 cup) plain
   (all-purpose) flour
2 eggs
2 tablespoons olive oil
lemon wedges, to serve

Roasted beetroot and potato salad
3 large beetroot (beets), trimmed
3 large desiree potatoes, peeled and
   cut into 2 cm (¾ inch) chunks
2 large handfuls baby rocket (arugula)
2 tablespoons balsamic vinegar
2 tablespoons extra virgin olive oil

Preheat the oven to 180°C (350°F/ Gas 4). To make the salad, wrap each beetroot in foil, place on a baking tray and bake for 1 hour. Put the potatoes on the same tray, distributed evenly. Bake for 30 minutes, or until tender.

Meanwhile, to prepare the schnitzels, place the fillets between two sheets of baking paper and flatten using a rolling pin. Combine the panko, herbs and lemon rind in a bowl. Place the flour in another bowl. In a third bowl, lightly beat the eggs. Dust the fillets with the flour, then dip into the egg, then the panko mixture. Place each piece on a plate and refrigerate until needed.

Remove the roasted beetroot and potato from the oven. Leave the beetroot until cool enough to handle, then peel off and discard the skins.

Heat the oil in a non-stick frying pan over medium heat. Add the schnitzels and fry in batches for 2–3 minutes on each side, or until cooked through. Drain on paper towels. Keep warm.

Meanwhile, cut the remaining beetroot into wedges and toss with the remaining potatoes, rocket, vinegar and olive oil. Divide the salad among serving plates. Top with the schnitzels and serve with lemon wedges.

Serves 4

Braised vegetables with cashews

1 tablespoon peanut oil
2 cloves garlic, crushed
2 teaspoons grated fresh ginger
300 g choy sum, cut into 10 cm
    lengths
150 g baby corn, sliced in half on the
    diagonal
185 ml (6 fl oz/¾ cup) chicken or
    vegetable stock
200 g tinned, drained bamboo shoots
150 g oyster mushrooms, sliced in half
2 teaspoons cornflour (cornstarch)
2 tablespoons oyster sauce
2 teaspoons sesame oil
90 g (3¼ oz/1 cup) bean sprouts
70 g (2½ oz) roasted unsalted
    cashews

Heat a wok over medium heat, add the oil and swirl to coat. Add the garlic and ginger and stir-fry for 1 minute. Increase the heat to high, add the choy sum and baby corn and stir-fry for another minute.

Add the chicken stock and cook for 3–4 minutes, or until the choy sum stems are just tender. Add the bamboo shoots and mushrooms, and cook for 1 minute.

Place the cornflour and 1 tablespoon water in a bowl and mix together well. Stir into the vegetables with the oyster sauce. Cook for 1–2 minutes, or until the sauce is slightly thickened. Stir in the sesame oil and sprouts, and serve immediately on a bed of steamed rice sprinkled with the roasted cashews.

Serves 4

Chicken and asparagus stir-fry

1 tablespoon oil
1 garlic clove, crushed
10 cm (4 inch) piece fresh ginger, peeled and thinly sliced
3 boneless, skinless chicken breasts, sliced
4 spring onions (scallions), sliced
200 g (7 oz/13 spears) asparagus, cut into short pieces
2 tablespoons soy sauce
40 g (1½ oz/⅓ cup) slivered almonds, roasted

Heat a wok or large frying pan over high heat, add the oil and swirl to coat. Add the garlic, ginger and chicken and stir-fry for 1–2 minutes, or until the chicken changes colour.

Add the spring onion and asparagus and stir-fry for a further 2 minutes, or until the spring onion is soft.

Stir in the soy sauce and 3 tablespoons water, cover and simmer for 2 minutes, or until the chicken is tender and the vegetables are slightly crisp. Sprinkle with the almonds and serve over steamed rice.

Serves 4

Thai jungle curry prawns

Curry paste
10–12 dried red chillies
4 red Asian shallots, chopped
4 cloves garlic, sliced
1 stem lemongrass, white part only,
 sliced
1 tablespoon finely chopped fresh
 galangal
2 small coriander (cilantro) roots,
 chopped
1 tablespoon finely chopped ginger
1 tablespoon shrimp paste, dry-
 roasted
60 ml (2 fl oz/¼ cup) oil
white pepper, to taste

1 tablespoon oil
1 garlic clove, crushed
40 g (1½ oz/¼ cup) ground
 candlenuts
1 tablespoon fish sauce
300 ml (10½ fl oz) fish stock
1 tablespoon whisky
600 g (1 lb 5 oz) raw prawns (shrimp),
 peeled, deveined, tails intact
1 small carrot, slivered
200 g (7 oz) snake (yard-long) beans,
 cut into 2 cm (¾ inch) lengths
50 g (1¾ oz) bamboo shoots
3 makrut (kaffir lime) leaves, crushed
fresh Thai basil leaves, to garnish

To make the curry paste, soak the
chillies in 250 ml (9 fl oz/1 cup) boiling
water for 10 minutes, then drain and
place in a food processor with the
remaining curry paste ingredients.
Season with salt and white pepper,
and process to a smooth paste.

Heat a wok over medium heat, add
the oil and stir to coat the side. Add
3 tablespoons of the curry paste and
the garlic and cook, stirring constantly,
for 5 minutes, or until fragrant. Stir in
the candlenuts, fish sauce, stock,
whisky, prawns, vegetables and lime
leaves, and bring to the boil. Reduce
the heat and simmer for 5 minutes,
or until the prawns and vegetables
are cooked through. Garnish with the
Thai basil leaves and freshly ground
black pepper.

Serves 6

Red curry of roast pumpkin, beans and basil

600 g (1 lb 5 oz) peeled and seeded
   pumpkin (winter squash), cut into
   3 cm (1¼ inch) cubes
2 tablespoons oil
1 tablespoon ready-made red curry
   paste
400 ml (14 fl oz) coconut cream
   (see Note)
200 g (7 oz) green beans, cut into
   3 cm (1¼ inch) lengths
2 makrut (kaffir lime) leaves, crushed
1 tablespoon grated light palm sugar
   (jaggery) or soft brown sugar
1 tablespoon fish sauce
2 large handfuls fresh Thai basil
   leaves, plus extra, to garnish
1 tablespoon lime juice

Preheat the oven to moderately hot
200°C (400°F/Gas 6). Place the
pumpkin in a baking dish with
1 tablespoon oil and toss to coat.
Bake for 20 minutes, or until tender.

Heat the remaining oil in a saucepan,
add the curry paste and cook, stirring
constantly, breaking up with a fork,
over medium heat for 1–2 minutes.
Add the coconut cream 125 ml
(4 fl oz/½ cup) at a time, stirring with
a wooden spoon between each
addition for a creamy consistency.
Then add the pumpkin and any
roasting juices, the beans and makrut
leaves. Reduce the heat to low and
cook for 5 minutes.

Stir in the palm sugar, fish sauce, basil
and lime juice. Garnish with extra basil
leaves. Serve with rice.

Serves 4

Note: If you want to make this a less
fattening meal, use lite coconut cream
instead of the full-fat version; the
texture will be slightly different but the
flavour of the curry will still be good.

Moroccan vegetable stew with minty couscous

2 tablespoons olive oil
1 onion, finely chopped
3 garlic cloves, finely chopped
1 teaspoon ground ginger
1 teaspoon ground turmeric
2 teaspoons ground cumin
2 teaspoons ground cinnamon
½ teaspoon dried chilli flakes
400 g (14 oz) tinned diced tomatoes
400 g (14 oz) tinned chickpeas, rinsed
  and drained
80 g (2¾ oz/½ cup) sultanas
400 g (14 oz) butternut pumpkin
  (squash), peeled and cut into 3 cm
  (1¼ inch) cubes
250 g (9 oz) zucchini (courgettes), cut
  into 2 cm (¾ inch) pieces
2 carrots, cut into 2 cm (¾ inch)
  pieces
185 g (6½ oz/i cup) instant couscous
25 g (1 oz) butter
4 tablespoons chopped mint

Heat the oil in a large saucepan over medium heat. Add the onion and cook for 3–5 minutes, or until translucent but not brown. Add the garlic, ginger, turmeric, cumin, cinnamon and chilli flakes, and cook for 1 minute. Add the tomato, chickpeas, sultanas and 250 ml (9 fl oz/1 cup) water. Bring to the boil, then reduce heat and simmer, covered, for 20 minutes. Add the pumpkin, zucchini and carrot, and cook for a further 20 minutes, or until the vegetables are tender. Season with salt and freshly ground black pepper.

Place the couscous in a large, heatproof bowl. Cover with 250 ml (9 fl oz/1 cup) boiling water and leave to stand for 5 minutes, or until all the water is absorbed. Fluff with a fork and stir in the butter and mint. Season with salt and freshly ground black pepper, and serve with the stew.

Serves 4

Root vegetable bake with crunchy cheesy almond crumbs

500 g (1 lb 2 oz) butternut pumpkin
   (squash), peeled and cut into 4 cm
   (1 1/2 inch) chunks
600 g (1 lb 5 oz) sweet potato, peeled
   and cut into 4 cm (1 1/2 inch) chunks
400 g (14 oz) sebago potatoes,
   peeled and cut into 4 cm (1 1/2 inch)
   chunks
2 parsnips, peeled and cut into 4 cm
   (1 1/2 inch) chunks
3 red onions
60 ml (2 fl oz/1/4 cup) olive oil
2 garlic cloves, chopped
1 small handful basil, plus extra, to
   garnish
2 tablespoons tomato paste
   (concentrated purée)
250 g (9 oz) cherry tomatoes
2 tablespoons pouring (whipping)
   cream
250 g (9 oz) Turkish bread, roughly
   chopped
100 g (3 1/2 oz/1 cup) grated parmesan
   cheese
65 g (2 1/2 oz/1/2 cup) grated gruyère
   cheese
80 g (2 3/4 oz/1/2 cup) blanched
   almonds, chopped
1 tablespoon oregano, chopped

Preheat the oven to 200°C (400°F/
Gas 6).

Put the pumpkin, sweet potato, potato
and parsnip in a large baking dish. Cut
two of the onions into wedges 1.5 cm
(5/8 inch) thick and add to the dish with
1 tablespoon of the olive oil. Toss to
coat the vegetables, then season with
sea salt and freshly ground black
pepper. Roast for 1 hour, or until the
vegetables are very tender.

Meanwhile, chop the remaining onion.
Place in a food processor with the
garlic, basil, tomato paste, tomatoes
and cream, then blend until a coarse
purée forms.

Put the bread in a bowl with the
parmesan, gruyère, almonds, oregano
and remaining oil. Mix together well.

Stir the puréed tomato mixture into
the roasted vegetables until well
coated, then scatter the breadcrumb
mixture over the top. Bake for a
further 30 minutes, or until the tomato
mixture is bubbling and the topping is
golden and crisp. Scatter with some
more basil and serve.

Serves 4

Spicy vegetable stew with dhal

Dhal
165 g (5¾ oz/¾ cup) yellow split peas
5 cm (2 inch) piece of fresh ginger,
  grated
2–3 garlic cloves, crushed
1 red chilli, seeded and chopped

3 tomatoes
2 tablespoons oil
1 teaspoon yellow mustard seeds
1 teaspoon cumin seeds
1 teaspoon ground cumin
½ teaspoon garam masala
1 red onion, cut into thin wedges
3 slender eggplants (aubergines),
  thickly sliced
2 carrots, thickly sliced
¼ cauliflower, cut into florets
375 ml (13 fl oz/1½ cups) vegetable
  stock
2 small zucchini (courgettes), thickly
  sliced
90 g (3¼ oz/½ cup) frozen peas
1 large handful coriander (cilantro)
  leaves

To make the dhal, put the split peas in a bowl, cover with water and soak for 2 hours. Drain. Place in a large saucepan with the ginger, garlic, chilli and 750 ml (26 fl oz/3 cups) water. Bring to the boil, reduce the heat and simmer for 45 minutes, or until soft.

Score a cross in the base of each tomato, soak in boiling water for 30 seconds, then plunge into cold water and peel the skin away from the cross. Cut in half and scoop out the seeds with a teaspoon. Chop the tomato flesh.

Heat the oil in a large saucepan. Cook the spices over medium heat for 30 seconds, or until fragrant. Add the onion and cook for 2 minutes, or until the onion is soft. Stir in the tomato, eggplant, carrot and cauliflower.

Add the dhal and stock, mix together well and simmer, covered, for 45 minutes, or until the vegetables are tender. Stir occasionally. Add the zucchini and peas during the last 10 minutes of cooking. Stir in the coriander leaves and serve hot.

Serves 4–6

Mushroom, ricotta and olive pizza

4 roma (plum) tomatoes, quartered
3/4 teaspoon caster (superfine) sugar
10 g (1/4 oz) dry yeast or 15 g (1/2 oz) fresh yeast
125 ml (4 fl oz/1/2 cup) skim milk
220 g (73/4 oz/13/4 cups) plain (all-purpose) flour
2 teaspoons olive oil
2 garlic cloves, crushed
1 onion, thinly sliced
750 g (1 lb 10 oz) mushrooms, sliced
250 g (9 oz/1 cup) low-fat ricotta cheese
2 tablespoons sliced black olives
small handful basil leaves

Preheat the oven to 210°C (415°F/ Gas 6–7). Put the tomato on a baking tray covered with baking paper, sprinkle with salt, pepper and 1/2 teaspoon sugar and bake for 20 minutes.

Stir the yeast and remaining sugar with 3 tablespoons warm water until the yeast dissolves. Cover and leave in a warm place until foamy. Warm the milk. Sift the flour into a bowl and stir in the yeast and milk. Mix to a soft dough, then turn onto a lightly floured surface and knead for 5 minutes. Leave, covered, in a lightly oiled bowl in a warm place for 40 minutes, or until doubled in size.

Heat the oil in a frying pan. Fry the garlic and onion until soft. Add the mushrooms and stir until the liquid has evaporated. Leave to cool.

Turn the dough out onto a lightly floured surface and knead lightly. Roll out to a 38 cm (15 inch) circle and transfer to a lightly greased pizza tray. Spread with the ricotta, leaving a border to turn over the filling. Top with the mushrooms, leaving a circle in the centre, and arrange the tomato and olives in the circle. Fold the dough edge over onto the mushroom and dust the edge with flour. Bake for 25 minutes, garnish with basil.

Serves 6

Chicken, artichoke and broad bean stew

60 g(2¼ oz/½ cup) plain (all-purpose)
    flour
8 chicken thighs on the bone, skin on
2 tablespoons olive oil
1 large red onion, cut into small
    wedges
125 ml (4 fl oz/½ cup) dry white wine
250 ml (9 fl oz/1 cup) chicken stock
2 teaspoons finely chopped rosemary
340 g (12 oz) jar of marinated
    artichoke hearts, drained well and
    cut into quarters
155 g (5½ oz/1 cup) frozen broad
    (fava) beans, peeled

Potato mash
800 g (1 lb 2 oz) potatoes. Peeled and
    cut into large chunks
60 g (2¼ oz) butter
3 tablespoons chicken stock

Season the flour with salt and pepper. Dust the chicken thighs in the flour, shaking off the excess. Heat the oil in a saucepan. Add the chicken in batches and brown over medium heat for 8 minutes, turning once. Remove. Drain on paper towel.

Add the onion to the pan and sauté for 3-4 minutes, or until softened but not browned. Increase the heat to high, add the wine and boil for 2 minutes, or until reduced to a syrupy consistency. Stir in the stock and bring the mixture just to the boil.

Return the chicken to the pan and add the rosemary. Reduce the heat to low, then cover and simmer for 45 minutes.

Add the artichoke, increase the heat to high and return to the boil. Reduce to a simmer and cook, uncovered, for 10-15 minutes. Add the beans and cook for a further 5 minutes.

Meanwhile, make the potato mash. Cook the potato in a saucepan of boiling salted water for 15-20 minutes, or until tender. Drain, then return to the pan. Add the butter and stock and mash well using a potato masher.

Spoon the mash into four bowls, then spoon the stew over to serve.

Serves 4

Broccoli and ricotta souffle

60 g (2¼ oz/1 cup) small broccoli
  florets
2 tablespoons olive oil
40 g (1½ oz) unsalted butter
1 onion, finely chopped
1 garlic clove, crushed
400 g (14 oz/scant 1⅔ cups) ricotta
  cheese
50 g (1¾ oz/½ cup) grated parmesan
  cheese
5 egg yolks, lightly beaten
a pinch of nutmeg
a pinch of cayenne pepper
5 egg whites
a pinch of cream of tartar
3 tablespoons dry breadcrumbs

Preheat the oven to 190°C (375°F/ Gas 5). Cook the broccoli florets in boiling salted water for 4 minutes, then drain well and roughly chop.

Heat the olive oil and butter in a frying pan. Add the onion and garlic and sauté over medium heat for 5 minutes, or until the onion has softened. Transfer to a large bowl and add the broccoli, ricotta, parmesan, egg yolks, nutmeg and cayenne pepper. Season with sea salt and freshly ground black pepper. Mix well.

In a clean, dry bowl, whisk the egg whites with the cream of tartar and a pinch of salt until stiff peaks form. Stir one-third of the beaten egg white into the broccoli mixture to loosen, then gently fold in the remaining egg white.

Grease a 1 litre (35 fl oz/4 cup) soufflé dish. Sprinkle with the breadcrumbs, turn the dish to coat, then shake out the excess. Spoon the broccoli mixture into the dish and bake for 35–40 minutes, or until puffed and golden brown. Serve immediately.

Serves 4

Note: Because this soufflé is based on ricotta cheese it won't rise as much as a conventional soufflé.

Mushroom quiche with parsley pastry

155 g (5½ oz/1¼ cups) plain (all-purpose) flour
3 tablespoons very finely chopped parsley
90 g (3¼ oz) cold unsalted butter, chopped
1 egg yolk, mixed with 2 tablespoons iced water

Mushroom filling
30 g (1 oz) unsalted butter
1 red onion, finely chopped
175 g (6 oz) button mushrooms, sliced
1 teaspoon lemon juice
4 tablespoons chopped parsley
3 tablespoons snipped chives
2 eggs, lightly beaten
170 ml (5½ fl oz/⅔ cup) pouring (whipping) cream

Sift the flour and a pinch of salt into a bowl. Mix the parsley through. Using your fingertips, rub the butter into the flour until the mixture resembles breadcrumbs. Make a well in the centre. Add the yolk mixture and mix using a flat-bladed knife until a rough dough forms. Turn out onto a floured surface and gather into a ball. Cover with wrap. Refrigerate for 30 minutes.

Roll out the pastry on a sheet of baking paper until large enough to fit the base and side of a 35 x 10 cm (14 x 4 inch) loose-based flan (tart) tin. Ease the pastry in and trim the edges. Refrigerate for 20 minutes.

Meanwhile, preheat the oven to 190°C (375°F/Gas 5). Line the pastry shell with baking paper and spread with a layer of baking beads. Bake the pastry for 15 minutes, then remove the paper and beads. Bake for 10 minutes. Lower the oven to 180°C (350°F/Gas 4).

To make the filling, melt the butter in a pan, add the onion. Sauté over medium heat for 5 minutes. Add the mushrooms. Sauté for 3 minutes. Stir in the juice and herbs. Meanwhile, mix the eggs and cream. Season. Spread the mushroom mixture into the pastry shell and pour the egg mixture over. Bake for 25–30 minutes. Serve warm.

Serves 4–6

Potato masala

2 tablespoons oil
1 teaspoon black mustard seeds
10 curry leaves
¼ teaspoon ground turmeric
1 cm (½ inch) piece of ginger, grated
2 green chillies, finely chopped
2 onions, chopped
500 g (1 lb 2 oz) waxy potatoes, cut
  into 2 cm (¾ inch) cubes
1 tablespoon tamarind purée

Heat the oil in a heavy-based frying pan, add the mustard seeds, cover, and when they start to pop add the curry leaves, turmeric, ginger, chilli and onion and cook, uncovered, until the onion is soft.

Add the potato cubes and 250 ml (9 fl oz/1 cup) water to the pan, bring to the boil, cover and cook until the potato is tender and almost breaking up. If there is any liquid left in the pan, let it simmer a little, uncovered, until it evaporates. If the potato isn't cooked and there is no liquid left, add a little more and continue to cook. Add the tamarind and season with salt.

Serves 4

Note: This filling is traditionally rolled in dosas — large pancakes made with rice flour — and served for breakfast or as a snack in southern India. However, it also makes an excellent spicy potato side dish.

Madras beef curry

1 tablespoon vegetable oil
2 onions, finely chopped
3 garlic cloves, finely chopped
1 tablespoon grated ginger
4 tablespoons madras curry paste
1 kg (2 lb 4 oz) chuck steak, trimmed
   and cut into 3 cm (1¼ inch) cubes
60 g (2¼ oz/¼ cup) tomato paste
   (concentrated purée)
250 ml (9 fl oz/1 cup) beef stock
6 new potatoes, halved
140 g (5 oz/1 cup) frozen peas

Preheat the oven to 180°C (350°F/ Gas 4). Heat the oil in a large heavy-based 3 litre (105 fl oz/12 cup) flameproof casserole dish. Cook the onion over medium heat for 4–5 minutes. Add the garlic and ginger and cook, stirring for 5 minutes, or until the onion is lightly golden, taking care not to burn it.

Add the curry paste and cook, stirring, for 2 minutes, or until fragrant. Increase the heat to high, add the meat and stir constantly for 2–3 minutes, or until the meat is well coated. Add the tomato paste and stock and stir well.

Bake, covered, for 50 minutes, stirring 2–3 times during cooking, and add a little water if necessary. Reduce the oven to 160°C (315°F/Gas 2–3). Add the potato and cook for 30 minutes, then add the peas and cook for another 10 minutes, or until the potato is tender. Serve hot with steamed jasmine rice.

Serves 6

Vegetarian paella

200 g (7 oz/1 cup) dried haricot beans
1/4 teaspoon saffron threads
2 tablespoons olive oil
1 onion, diced
1 red capsicum (pepper), cut into
   1 x 4 cm (1/2 x 1 1/2 inch) strips
5 garlic cloves, crushed
275 g (9¾ oz/1 1/4 cups) paella or
   arborio rice
1 tablespoon sweet paprika
1/2 teaspoon mixed spice
750 ml (26 fl oz/3 cups) vegetable
   stock
400 g (14 oz) tinned chopped
   tomatoes
1 1/2 tablespoons tomato paste
   (concentrated purée)
150 g (5 1/2 oz) fresh or frozen soya
   beans (see Note)
100 g (3 1/2 oz) silverbeet (Swiss chard)
   leaves (no stems), shredded
400 g (14 oz) can artichoke hearts,
   drained and quartered
4 tablespoons chopped coriander
   (cilantro) leaves

Put the haricot beans in a bowl, cover with cold water and soak overnight. Drain and rinse well. Place the saffron threads in a small frying pan over medium–low heat. Dry-fry, shaking the pan, for 1 minute, or until darkened. Remove from the heat and, when cool, crumble into a small bowl. Pour in 125 ml (4 fl oz/1/2 cup) warm water and allow to steep.

Heat the oil in a large paella or frying pan. Add the onion and capsicum and cook over medium–high heat for 4–5 minutes, or until the onion is soft. Stir in the garlic and cook for 1 minute. Reduce the heat and add the beans, rice, paprika, mixed spice and 1/2 teaspoon salt. Stir to coat. Add the saffron water, stock, tomato and tomato paste and bring to the boil. Cover, reduce the heat and simmer for 20 minutes.

Stir in the soya beans, silverbeet and artichoke hearts and cook, covered, for 8 minutes, or until all the liquid is absorbed and the rice and beans are tender. Turn off the heat and leave for 5 minutes. Stir in the coriander just before serving.

Serves 6

Note: Fresh or frozen soya beans are available from Asian grocery stores.

Shepherd's pie topped with pea and potato mash

2 tablespoons olive oil
2 carrots, finely chopped
1 large onion, finely chopped
1 large celery stalk, finely chopped
2 garlic cloves, chopped
800 g (1 lb 12 oz) minced (ground) lamb
375 ml (13 fl oz/1½ cups) beef stock
2 tablespoons tomato paste (concentrated purée)
1 tablespoon worcestershire sauce
2 thyme sprigs
1 tablespoon plain (all-purpose) flour
3 tablespoons chopped parsley

Pea and potato mash
750 g (1 lb 10 oz) desiree potatoes, peeled and cut into 5 cm (2 inch) chunks
310 g (11 oz/2¼ cups) frozen peas
40 g (1½ oz) butter, plus some extra melted butter for brushing
2 tablespoons milk

Preheat the oven to 200°C (400°F /Gas 6). Heat the oil in a pan over medium heat. Sauté the vegetables and garlic for 5 minutes. Increase the heat to high. Add the lamb and stir for 5–7 minutes until the meat has changed colour. Break up lumps with a wooden spoon. Stir in the stock, paste and sauce. Add the sprigs.

Bring to the boil, reduce the heat and simmer, stirring, for 20–25 minutes. Stir in the flour. Cook for 5 minutes. Remove the sprigs, then stir in the parsley and season. Spoon the mixture into a 2 litre (70 fl oz/8 cup) baking dish.

While the lamb is simmering, make the mash topping. Cook the potatoes in a saucepan of boiling salted water for 15 minutes. In a separate saucepan of boiling salted water, cook the peas for 3 minutes. Drain the potatoes and peas. Mash the potatoes with the butter and milk and season well. Put the peas in a food processor and blend to a smooth purée, then mix through the potato mash.

Spread the mash over the lamb mixture. Use a fork to roughen the surface. Brush the topping with melted butter. Bake for 20 minutes, or until the topping is golden brown. Allow to cool slightly, then serve.

Serves 4

Stuffed baked potatoes

4 large potatoes (150 g/5½ oz each), such as king edward, sebago or desiree

Bacon, cheese and creamed corn topping
4 slices of bacon, chopped
125 g (4½ oz) tinned creamed corn
60 g (2¼ oz/½ cup) grated cheddar cheese
2 tablespoons finely snipped chives

Ricotta, baby spinach and ham topping
1 tablespoon olive oil
1 small red onion, finely chopped
80 g (2¾ oz/½ cup) chopped leg ham
50 g (1¾ oz) baby English spinach leaves
160 g (5½ oz/⅔ cup) fresh, firm ricotta cheese
3 spring onions (scallions), finely sliced

Chorizo, tomato and olive topping
2 chorizo sausages, chopped
2 tomatoes, chopped
40 g (1½ oz/¼ cup) pitted kalamata olives, chopped
2 tablespoons chopped basil
50 g (1¾ oz/⅓ cup) crumbled feta cheese

Preheat the oven to 200°C (400°F/ Gas 6). Wash and dry the potatoes, pierce them with a fork, then wrap each one in foil. Bake for 1 hour.

Just before the potatoes are cooked, prepare your desired toppings. For the bacon topping, cook the bacon in a non–stick frying pan over medium heat for 3 minutes. Remove from the heat and drain on paper towels. Meanwhile, heat the creamed corn in a small saucepan until warm. Transfer to a bowl, stir in the bacon and cheese and sprinkle with the chives.

For the ricotta topping, heat the oil in a frying pan over medium heat, add the onion and cook for 2 minutes. Remove from the heat and place in a bowl. Add the ham, spinach and ricotta. Mix and sprinkle with the onion.

For the chorizo topping, place the chorizo in a frying pan over medium heat and cook for 5 minutes. Add the tomatoes and olives and cook for 2 minutes. Transfer to a bowl and sprinkle with the basil and feta.

When the potatoes are ready cut a cross into the top of each. Squeeze them around the middle with your fingers to push open the potatoes. Serve with your choice of topping.

Serves 4

Welsh lamb and vegetable pie

750 g (1 lb 10 oz) boned lamb
  shoulder, cubed
90 g (3¼ oz/¾ cup) plain (all-purpose)
  flour, seasoned
2 tablespoons olive oil
200 g (7 oz) bacon, finely chopped
2 garlic cloves, chopped
4 large leeks, sliced
1 large carrot, chopped
2 large potatoes, cut into 1 cm
  (½ inch) cubes
310 ml (10¾ oz/1¼ cups) beef stock
1 bay leaf
2 teaspoons chopped flat-leaf (Italian)
  parsley
375 g (13 oz) puff pastry
1 egg, lightly beaten

Toss the meat in the seasoned flour and shake off the excess. Heat the oil in a large frying pan over medium heat. Cook the meat in batches for 4–5 minutes, or until well browned, then remove from the pan. Add the bacon and cook for 3 minutes. Add the garlic and leek and cook for about 5 minutes, or until the leek is soft.

Put the meat in a large saucepan, add the leek and bacon, carrot, potato, stock and bay leaf and bring to the boil, then reduce the heat, cover and simmer for 30 minutes. Uncover and simmer for 1 hour, or until the meat is cooked and the liquid has thickened. Season. Remove the bay leaf, stir in the parsley and set aside to cool.

Preheat the oven to 200°C (400°F/ Gas 6). Divide the filling among four 375 ml (13 fl oz/1½ cups) pie dishes. Divide the pastry into four and roll each piece out between two sheets of baking paper until large enough to cover the pie. Remove the top sheet of paper and invert the pastry over the filling. Trim the edges and pinch to seal. Cut two slits in the top for steam to escape. Brush with egg and bake for 45 minutes, or until the pastry is crisp and golden.

Serves 6

Fried beef with potato, peas and ginger

oil, for deep-frying
1 potato, cut into small cubes
2.5 cm (1 inch) piece of ginger
500 g (1 lb 2 oz) beef rump steak,
  thinly sliced
3 garlic cloves, crushed
1 teaspoon ground black pepper
2 tablespoons oil, extra
2 onions, sliced in rings
60 ml (2 fl oz/¼ cup) beef stock
2 tablespoons tomato paste
  (concentrated purée)
½ tablespoon soy sauce
1 teaspoon chilli powder
3 tablespoons lemon juice
3 tomatoes, chopped
50 g (1¾ oz/⅓ cup) fresh or frozen
  peas

Fill a deep heavy-based saucepan one-third full with oil and heat to 180°C (350°F/Gas 4), or until a cube of bread dropped in the oil browns in 15 seconds. Deep-fry the potato cubes until golden brown. Drain on paper towels.

Pound the ginger using a mortar and pestle, or grate with a fine grater into a bowl. Put the ginger into a piece of muslin, twist it up tightly and squeeze out all the juice (you will need about 1 tablespoon).

Put the steak in a bowl, add the garlic, pepper and ginger juice and toss well. Heat the oil and fry the beef quickly in batches over high heat. Keep each batch warm as you remove it. Reduce the heat, fry the onions until golden, then remove.

Put the stock, tomato paste, soy sauce, chilli powder and lemon juice in the saucepan and cook over medium heat until reduced. Add the fried onion, cook for 3 minutes, add the chopped tomato and the peas, then stir well and cook for 1 minute. Add the beef and potato and toss well until heated through.

Serves 4

Pasta with artichokes and grilled chicken

1 tablespoon olive oil
3 boneless, skinless chicken breasts
500 g (1 lb 2 oz) pasta, such as
    tagliatelle or any long, flat pasta
8 slices prosciutto
280 g (10 oz) jar artichokes in oil,
    drained and quartered, oil reserved
150 g (5½ oz) semi-dried (sun-
    blushed) tomatoes, thinly sliced
90 g (3¼ oz) baby rocket (arugula)
    leaves
2–3 tablespoons balsamic vinegar

Lightly brush a chargrill pan (griddle) or frying pan with oil and heat over high heat. Cook the chicken breasts for 6–8 minutes each side, or until they are cooked through. Thinly slice and set aside.

Cook the pasta in a large saucepan of boiling salted water until *al dente*. Drain the pasta and return to the pan to keep warm. Meanwhile, place the prosciutto under a hot grill (broiler) and grill (broil) for 2 minutes each side, or until crisp. Cool slightly and break into pieces.

Combine the pasta with the chicken, prosciutto, artichokes, tomato and rocket in a bowl and toss. Whisk together 60 ml (2 fl oz/¼ cup) of the reserved artichoke oil and the balsamic vinegar and toss through the pasta mixture. Season and serve.

Serves 6

Penne with spring vegetables and pesto

Basil pesto
225 g (8 oz) basil
80 g (2¾ oz/½ cup) pine nuts
1 garlic clove, roughly chopped
30 g (1 oz/⅓ cup) grated pecorino
  cheese, plus extra, to serve
1 red chilli, roughly chopped
185 ml (6 fl oz/¾ cup) olive oil

200 g (7 oz) broccoli, chopped into
  florets
100 g (3½ oz) button mushrooms,
  sliced
1 carrot, cut into thin strips
175 g (6 oz/10 spears) asparagus,
  trimmed and cut into 2 cm (¾ inch)
  lengths
500 g (1 lb 2 oz) penne
½ red capsicum (pepper), cut into thin
  strips

To make the pesto, put the basil, pine nuts, garlic, pecorino and chilli in a food processor and blend until finely chopped. With motor running, add the olive oil in a thin stream and process until well combined. Season to taste.

Line a large steamer with baking paper and punch with holes. Arrange the broccoli, mushrooms, carrot and asparagus in a single layer on top and cover with a lid. Sit the steamer over a saucepan or wok of simmering water and steam for about 4–5 minutes, or until just cooked.

Meanwhile, cook the penne in a large saucepan of rapidly boiling salted water for 10 minutes, or until *al dente*. Drain well and return to the pan. Add steamed vegetables, capsicum and pesto and mix well. Serve hot or cold with extra pecorino.

Serves 4

Capsicum, snowpea and hokkien noodle stir-fry

500 g (1 lb 2 oz) hokkien (egg)
    noodles
1 tablespoon vegetable or peanut oil
1 red onion, cut into thin wedges
2 garlic cloves, crushed
3 cm (1¼ inch) piece fresh ginger,
    thinly sliced
150 g (5½ oz) snowpeas (mangetout),
    topped and tailed, large ones halved
    on the diagonal
1 carrot, halved lengthways, sliced on
    the diagonal
1 red capsicum (pepper), thinly sliced
4 tablespoons Chinese barbecue
    sauce (char siu sauce)
1 handful coriander (cilantro) leaves

Soak the noodles in boiling water for 5 minutes to soften and separate; drain well.

Heat a wok over high heat, add oil and swirl to coat. Add onion, garlic and ginger and stir-fry for 1 minute. Add snowpeas, carrot and capsicum and cook for 2–3 minutes. Stir in the noodles and barbecue sauce; cook for a further 2 minutes. Toss in the coriander leaves and serve.

Serves 4

Green lentil and vegetable curry

1 teaspoon canola oil
1 large onion, chopped
2 garlic cloves, chopped
1–2 tablespoons curry paste
1 teaspoon ground turmeric
200 g (7 oz/1 cup) green lentils, rinsed
and drained
1.25 litres (44 fl oz/5 cups) vegetable
stock or water
1 large carrot, cut into 2 cm (3/4 inch)
cubes
2 potatoes, cut into 2 cm (3/4 inch)
cubes
250 g (9 oz) sweet potato, peeled and
cut into 2 cm (3/4 inch) cubes
350 g (12 oz) cauliflower, broken into
small florets
150 g (5½ oz) green beans, trimmed
and halved
basil, to serve
coriander (cilantro) leaves, to serve

Heat oil in a saucepan over a medium heat. Add the onion and garlic, and cook for 3 minutes, or until softened. Stir in the curry paste and turmeric and stir for 1 minute. Add the lentils and stock or water.

Bring to a boil, then reduce the heat. Cover and simmer for 30 minutes, then add the carrot, potatoes and sweet potato. Simmer, covered, for 20 minutes, or until the lentils and vegetables are tender.

Add the cauliflower and beans once most of the liquid has been absorbed. Remove lid and simmer for a further few minutes if there is too much liquid.

Serve hot with brown or basmati rice and top with basil and coriander.

Serves 4

Curried eggplant stir-fry

2 tablespoons vegetable oil
½–1 long green chilli, finely sliced
4 red Asian shallots, chopped
2 garlic cloves, finely sliced
2 tablespoons rogan josh masala
  curry paste or mild curry paste
350 g (12 oz) slender eggplants
  (aubergines), cut on the diagonal
  into 1 cm (½ inch) slices
3 vine-riped tomatoes, each cut into
  8 wedges
70 g (2½ oz) baby English spinach
  leaves

Heat oil in a large wok and swirl to coat. Add green chilli, shallots and garlic and stir-fry over high heat for 1 minute. Stir in the curry paste and stir-fry for 1 minute.

Add eggplant and stir-fry 3 minutes, or until the eggplant has softened a little. Add the tomato and 125 ml (4 fl oz/½ cup) of water. Cover the wok and cook for 10 minutes, or until the eggplant is cooked, stirring occasionally. Stir in the spinach leaves and cook for 1 minute, or until wilted. Serve immediately.

Serves 4

Layered country cob

2 red capsicums (peppers)
1 eggplant (aubergine), thinly sliced
1 large red onion, thinly sliced
450 g (1 lb) white cob loaf
1 tablespoon olive oil
2 garlic cloves, finely chopped
1 teaspoon chopped lemon thyme
250 g (9 oz) English spinach
350 g (12 oz) ricotta cheese

Preheat the grill (broiler) to hot. Cut the capsicum in quarters lengthways and remove the seeds and membrane. Arrange the capsicum, skin side up, and the eggplant, sprayed lightly with oil, on the grill. Grill (broil) for about 7 minutes, turning the eggplant over as it browns and until the capsicum skin is blackened and blistered, then leave to cool. Grill the onion for about 6 minutes, turning once, until soft. Slip the skin off the capsicum.

Cut the top off the cob and pull out the centre. Combine the oil, garlic and thyme and brush lightly inside the shell. Put the spinach leaves in a bowl and pour boiling water over to cover. Allow to soften for 1 minute, rinse with cold water until cool, then drain and pat dry with paper towels.

To fill the cob, arrange half the eggplant in the base, followed by capsicum and onion, then a layer of ricotta, spinach and the remaining eggplant. Season between layers. Press down firmly. If the top of the cob is empty, fill the space with a little of the soft bread from the centre. Replace the top of the loaf and wrap the whole thing securely with foil. Top with a brick wrapped in foil to weigh it down. Refrigerate overnight. Cut into wedges to serve.

Serves 8

Prosciutto and vegetable pasta bake

3 tablespoons olive oil
35 g (1¼ oz/⅓ cup) dried
  breadcrumbs
250 g (9 oz) pasta shapes
6 thin slices prosciutto, chopped
1 red onion, chopped
1 red capsicum (pepper), chopped
100 g (3½ oz/½ cup) semi-dried (sun-
  blushed) tomatoes, roughly chopped
3 tablespoons shredded basil
100 g (3½ oz/1 cup) grated parmesan
  cheese
4 eggs, lightly beaten
250 ml (9 fl oz/1 cup) milk

Preheat the oven to 180°C (350°F/
Gas 4). Grease a 25 cm (10 inch)
round ovenproof dish with a little of
the olive oil and sprinkle the dish with
2 tablespoons of the breadcrumbs to
coat the base and side. Cook the
pasta in a large saucepan of boiling
water until *al dente*. Drain and transfer
to a large bowl.

Heat 1 tablespoon of the remaining
oil in a large frying pan. Add the
prosciutto and onion and cook over
medium heat for 4–5 minutes, or until
softened and golden in colour. Add
the capsicum and semi-dried tomato
and cook for a further 1–2 minutes.
Add to the pasta with the basil and
parmesan and toss together. Spoon
the mixture into the prepared dish.

Place the eggs and milk in a bowl,
whisk together, then season with salt
and freshly ground black pepper. Pour
the egg mixture over the pasta.
Season the remaining breadcrumbs,
add the remaining oil and toss
together. Sprinkle the seasoned
breadcrumb mixture over the pasta.
Bake for 40 minutes, or until set. Allow
to stand for 5 minutes, then cut into
wedges and serve with a green salad,
if desired.

Serves 6–8

Baked eggs

80 ml (2½ fl oz/⅓ cup) olive oil
400 g (14 oz) potatoes, cut into 2 cm
 (¾ in) cubes
1 red capsicum (pepper), cut into thin
 strips
1 brown onion, chopped
100 g (3½ oz) thinly sliced jamón or
 prosciutto
150 g (5½ oz/9 spears) thin green
 asparagus, trimmed
100 g (3½ oz) fresh or frozen green
 peas
100 g (3½ oz) baby green beans,
 sliced
500 g (1 lb 2 oz) ripe tomatoes,
 peeled, seeded and chopped
2 tablespoons tomato paste
 (concentrated purée)
4 eggs
100 g (3½ oz) chorizo, thinly sliced
2 tablespoons chopped flat-leaf
 (Italian) parsley

Heat the oil in a large frying pan and cook the potato over medium heat for 8 minutes, or until golden. Remove with a slotted spoon. Reduce the heat and add the capsicum and onion to the pan. Cut two of the jamón slices into pieces similar in size to the capsicum and add to the pan. Cook for 6 minutes, or until the onion is soft.

Preheat oven to 180°C (350°F/Gas 4). Reserve four asparagus spears. Add rest to pan with peas, beans, tomato and tomato paste. Stir in 125 ml (4 fl oz/½ cup) water and season well with salt and freshly ground black pepper. Return the potato to the pan. Cover and cook over low heat for 10 minutes, stirring occasionally.

Grease a large oval ovenproof dish. Transfer the vegetables to the dish, discarding any excess liquid. Using the back of a spoon, make four deep, evenly spaced indentations and break an egg into each. Top with the reserved asparagus and the chorizo. Cut the remaining jamón into large pieces and distribute over the top. Sprinkle with parsley. Bake for about 20 minutes, or until the egg whites are just set. Serve warm.

Serves 4

Tagine omelette with tomatoes

2 tablespoons olive oil
1 white onion, finely chopped
1 teaspoon ground coriander
1 teaspoon paprika
pinch of cayenne pepper
2 x 400 g (14 oz) tinned roma (plum)
  tomatoes, chopped
3 tablespoons chopped flat-leaf
  (Italian) parsley
3 tablespoons chopped coriander
  (cilantro) leaves, extra to serve
8 eggs

Use a 25–28 cm (10–11¼ in) non-stick frying pan with a domed lid to fit. Place over low–medium heat and add oil and onion. Cook for 6 minutes or until onion is soft. Stir in the spices and cook for a further 2 minutes. Add tomatoes and their liquid, and the parsley. Increase heat to medium, season and allow to simmer, uncovered until sauce is reduced and thick – about 10 minutes.

Break eggs into a bowl and add 2 tablespoons water. Season and beat lightly with a fork; enough to mix whites and yolks. Pour eggs over the back of a large spoon so that the mixture evenly covers the sauce. Cover with the lid and cook over medium heat for 15 minutes. Scatter with coriander leaves and serve, either cut into wedges, or spooned onto plates. Serve with bread.

To cook in a tagine: Make the tomato sauce in a frying pan. Remove shelves in oven, leaving the bottom shelf. Preheat oven to 180°C (350°F/Gas 4). Transfer hot, cooked sauce to the tagine, cover and place in oven for 10 minutes. Remove tagine from oven, immediately pour beaten eggs over the sauce, cover with its lid and return to oven for 5–8 minutes until omelette is set. Serve from the tagine.

Serves 4

Potato omelette

500 g (1 lb 2 oz) all-purpose potatoes,
  peeled and cut into 1 cm (½ inch)
  slices
60 ml (2 fl oz/¼ cup) olive oil
1 brown onion, thinly sliced
4 garlic cloves, thinly sliced
2 tablespoons finely chopped flat-leaf
  (Italian) parsley
6 eggs

Put the potato slices in a large
saucepan, cover with cold water
and bring to the boil over high heat.
Boil for 5 minutes, then drain and
set aside.

Heat the oil in a deep-sided non-stick
frying pan over medium heat. Add
the onion and garlic and cook for
5 minutes, or until the onion softens.

Add the potato and parsley to the
pan and stir to combine. Cook over
medium heat for 5 minutes, gently
pressing down into the pan.

Whisk the eggs with 1 teaspoon
each of salt and freshly ground black
pepper and pour evenly over the
potato. Cover and cook over low–
medium heat for 20 minutes, or until
the eggs are just set. Slide onto a
serving plate or serve directly from
the pan.

Serves 6–8

Scrambled eggs with asparagus

2 garlic cloves, chopped
1 thick slice bread, crusts removed
60 ml (2 fl oz/¼ cup) olive oil
175 g (6 oz/10 spears) asparagus, cut
    into 2 cm (¾ inch) lengths
1 teaspoon sweet paprika (pimentón)
2 tablespoons white wine vinegar
6 eggs, beaten

Put the garlic and bread in a food processor or mortar and pestle and grind to a loose paste, adding a small amount of water (1–2 tablespoons).

Heat the oil in a frying pan and sauté the asparagus over medium heat for 2 minutes, or until just starting to become tender. Add the garlic and bread paste, paprika, vinegar and a pinch of salt, and stir to combine. Cover and cook over medium heat for 2–3 minutes, or until the asparagus is tender.

Pour in the eggs and stir for a few minutes. Remove the mixture from the heat just before it is fully cooked (the perfect revuelto is creamy in consistency), then season to taste and serve immediately.

Serves 4

INDEX

INDEX

INDEX

INDEX

INDEX

Published in 2011 by Murdoch Books Pty Limited

Murdoch Books Australia
Pier 8/9, 23 Hickson Road
Millers Point NSW 2000
Phone: +61 (0)2 8220 2000
Fax: +61 (0)2 8220 2558
www.murdochbooks.com.au

Murdoch Books UK Limited
Erico House, 6th Floor
93-99 Upper Richmond Road
Putney, London SW15 2TG
Phone: +44 (0)20 8785 5995
Fax: +44 (0)20 8785 5985
www.murdochbooks.co.uk

Designer: Transformer
Photography (cover): Stuart Scott
Stylist (cover): Louise Bickle
Production: Joan Beal

National Library of Australia Cataloguing-in-Publication entry
Title: Chunky vegetables.
ISBN: 9781742667225 (pbk.)
Notes: Includes index.
Subjects: Cooking (Vegetables)
Vegetarian cooking.
Dewey Number: 641.65

Printed by 1010 Printing International Limited, China
PRINTED IN CHINA

Cover credits: All fabrics from No Chintz, Sydney.

IMPORTANT: Those who might be at risk from the effects of salmonella poisoning (the elderly,
pregnant women, young children and those suffering from immune deficiency diseases)
should consult their doctor with any concerns about eating raw eggs.

OVEN GUIDE: You may find cooking times vary depending on the oven you are using. For fan-forced
ovens, as a general rule, set the oven temperature to 20°C (35°F) lower than indicated in the recipe.